# MINISTERING ANGEL

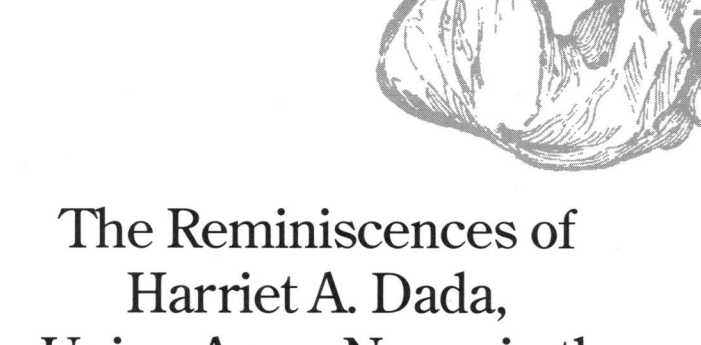

The Reminiscences of
Harriet A. Dada,
a Union Army Nurse in the
Civil War

Edmund J. Raus, Jr.

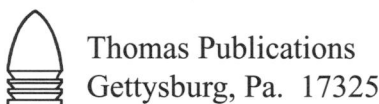

Thomas Publications
Gettysburg, Pa. 17325

Copyright © 2004 Edmund J. Raus, Jr.
Printed and bound in the United States of America
Published by THOMAS PUBLICATIONS
P.O. Box 3031
Gettysburg, Pa. 17325
All rights reserved. No part of this book may be used or reproduced without written permission of the author and the publisher, except in the case of brief quotations embodied in critical essays and reviews.
ISBN-1-57747-099-0

# Introduction

Harriet A. Dada of Oswego and Cortland counties in upstate New York was one of the estimated 3,214[1] army nurses that served in the hospitals, on medical ships, or in the field with the Union armies during the Civil War. For four long years these dedicated and determined women battled against the ever-present hand of death, the ravages of camp disease, and the unsanitary and disorganized conditions of the military hospitals. They endured incredible hardships, low pay,[2] poor rations, and at times the prejudices of many male surgeons and hospital administrators who denigrated their efforts with "unkind words and sneers." In the end, however, their outstanding record of achievement not only saved many lives during the war but also afterwards opened many doors to American women desiring to enter the medical profession.

Before the war, nursing was considered no place for the refined sensibilities of "proper" American women.[3] Female "nurses" in public hospitals were essentially charwomen, servants, or cooks who came from the ranks of the lower classes and at times were recruited from the poor houses and prisons. No schools existed in America to train nurses outside of the Catholic orders whose sister nurses provided staffing for the existing 28 Catholic hospitals.[4] America produced no women doctors until Elizabeth Blackwell (1821–1910) received her medical degree from the Geneva (N.Y.) Medical College in 1849.

By the 1880s however, stemming in part from the accomplishments of the Civil War nurses, 22 nursing schools were in operation while countless women physicians made a mark for themselves in the profession. In 1892 Congress belatedly acknowledged the service of Civil War nurses by passing the Army Nurse Pension

---

1. The figure represents the category of nurses like Dada who were appointed and paid by the government. Sister Mary Denis Maher, *To Bind Up the Wounds, Catholic Sister Nurses in the U.S. Civil War* (Baton Rouge: Louisiana State University Press, 1999), p. 51.
2. By act of Congress in August of 1861 female nurses while in service were to receive forty cents a day, one ration, and transportation. *General Orders Affecting The Volunteer Force; Adjutant General's Office, 1861* (Government Printing Office, Washington, D. C., 1862), p. 22.
3. Marilyn Mayer Culpepper, *Trials and Triumphs: The Women Of The American Civil War* (East Lansing: Michigan State University Press, 1991), pp. 315-16.
4. Maher, *To Bind Up the Wounds*, pp. 28, 38; Sylvia G.L. Dannett, ed., *Noble Women of the North* (New York: Thomas Yoseloff, 1959), p. 55.

*Harriet Dada.*

Act, which gave the women the status of military veterans able to seek federal pensions on proof of service. Altogether 2,448 women applied for a federal pension; many, perhaps, seeking as much the recognition of their Civil War service as the 12 dollars a month pension payment.[5]

Harriet A. Dada was one of a number of former army nurses who wrote down their Civil war experience. For over four years Dada had cared for the sick and wounded soldiers at a number of military hospitals in both the Eastern and Western theaters of the war. Although she did not keep a daily journal, she saved her letters from the field. These letters were first used for the short biographical sketches of her and nurse Susan Hall in the book *Woman's Work in the Civil War*, published in 1867.[6] In 1884 her letters provided the basis for her ten part series of articles reproduced here and originally published in the *National Tribune* newspaper under the heading "Ministering Angels." These reminiscences provide a historically significant and poignant story of a woman's self-sacrifice, devotion to duty and struggle in the face of great adversity. Although she received little official recognition or reward for her years of army service, she did not look back on that period of her life with any apparent feeling of regret or rancor. "Surely," she wrote in 1884, "I did receive my reward. ...it had been my privilege to minister to the sick and wounded soldiers—one of the greatest privileges given to an American woman."

Actually, Dada's Civil War service was just one episode in her full life of service. Her father Lemuel Dada, a cabinetmaker and minister, settled in Cortland County, New York, early in the century where he married Merinda Budlong in 1822. They had three children: Samuel Newell Dada, b. 1826; Elizabeth, b. around 1832; and Harriet, born 1835 in Hannibal, Oswego County, New York. At age ten Harriet moved with her family to Fulton, New York where she attended local schools and graduated in 1854 from the local academy, later Falley Seminary. At age 20 she became a teacher to the Choctaw Indians under the auspices of the American Board of Commissioners for Foreign Missions. She proved adept at learning the Choctaw language, earning the Indian name

---

5. Mary Gardner Holland, *Our Army Nurses; Stories from Women in the Civil War, with an introduction by Daniel John Hoisington* (Roseville, Minnesota: Edinborough Press, 1998), p. ii.
6. Linus Pierpont Brockett, M.D.and Mrs. Mary C. Vaughan, with an introduction by Henry W. Bellows, D.D., *Woman's Work In The Civil War: A Record of Heroism, Patriotism and Patience* (Philadelphia: Zeigler, McCurdy & Co., 1867), pp. 431-9.

"Imponna," meaning skillful. During the winter of 1860, threats and hostile actions by local pro-Southern individuals forced Dada and other Northern teachers to leave their station and return home, traveling discreetly overland to reach the railroad at St. Joseph, Missouri. She was living with her father in Fulton, anticipating a return to the Indian Territory, when the Confederates fired upon Fort Sumter.[7]

When the Civil War began, women throughout the North stepped forward to offer their services for the war effort. Many, inspired by the tales of Florence Nightingale's volunteer nurses during the Crimean War, thought nursing an appropriate outlet for their patriotism and a natural extension of their traditional nurturing role of family caregiver. Some, no doubt, also saw nursing as an opportunity for adventure and a chance to share in the trials and successes of their loved ones in uniform. Doctor Elizabeth Blackwell, a founder and director of the New York Infirmary for Women and Children in New York City, assumed a prominent role in channeling the patriotic enthusiasms of Northern women toward meeting the medical and relief needs of the thousands of Northern volunteers entering military service. In late April 1861 at least 2,000 eager female spectators attended an organizational meeting at Cooper Institute in New York City to witness the creation of the Women's Central Association of Relief (WCAR), a forerunner of the more prominent Sanitary Commission.[8]

Blackwell spearheaded the program of the WCAR to register and examine the would-be Florence Nightingales that sought positions as volunteer nurses. The WCAR sponsored their training in New York City hospitals and then referred them to Dorothea Lynde Dix (1802–1887), the prominent reformer who at the time held the appointment as superintendent of the United States Army Nurses with headquarters in Washington D.C. By November 1861, 32 WCAR nurses were serving in the military hospitals in and around Washington.[9] One of them was Harriet Dada.

Dada responded to one of the first calls for army nurses. In her application she received the endorsement of the prominent Homer,

---

7. Dada genealogical file, Cortland County Historical Society, Cortland, New York. File mentions that Lemuel, b. 1796 in Southampton, Massachusetts, had lived in Homer, New York before coming to Cortland in 1825. He was one of the first trustees of the Presbyterian Church in Cortland; Dwight H. Bruce, ed., *Onondaga's Centennial. Gleanings Of A Century* (The Boston History Company. Publishers. 1896), Vol. II, Part III, "Family Sketches," p. 15.
8. Judith Ann Giesberg, *Civil War Sisterhood; The U.S. Sanitary Commission and Women's Politics in Transition* (Boston: Northeastern University Press, 2000), p. 33.
9. *Ibid*, p. 41.

New York, doctor and educator Caleb Green who certified her as "eminently qualified for the duties of Hospital Nurse." Once accepted for training, Dada spent six weeks listening to lectures by prominent surgeons in New York City and working as a nurse at Bellevue hospital.[10] Two days after the First Battle of Bull Run she and her good friend and fellow missionary to the Indians Susan Hall arrived in Washington to be immediately plunged into the task at hand by the terse directive of Dorothea Dix: "You are needed in Alexandria."

The following are Dada's places of service.

| | |
|---|---|
| July 23, 1861 – April 1, 1862 | Alexandria, Virginia |
| April 1, 1862 – May 22, 1862 | Winchester, Virginia |
| May 22 – 23, 1862 | Strasburg, Virginia |
| May 23, 1862 – July 12, 1862 | Winchester, Virginia |
| July 12, 1862 – August 23, 1862 | Harpers Ferry, Virginia |
| August 23, 1862 – November 8, 1862 | Washington, D.C. |
| November 8, 1862 – May 22, 1863 | Harpers Ferry, Virginia |
| May 22, 1863 – June 14, 1863 | Aquia Creek, Virginia |
| June 14, 1863 – July 8, 1863 | Washington, D.C. |
| July 8, 1863 – October 23, 1863 | Gettysburg, Pennsylvania |
| December 3, 1863 – May 22, 1864 | Murfreesboro, Tennessee |
| May 22, 1864 – September 19, 1865 | Chattanooga, Tennessee |

Dada indicates that her various duties in the hospitals included organizing and administering hospital stores, preparing special diets, providing a primary link between patients and their families, and generally ministering to the physical and spiritual needs of her charges. Although in her narrative she does not hesitate to criticize several incompetent surgeons and hospital administrators that she encountered, she apparently managed to maintain a strictly professional relationship with both colleagues and patients. Only once, for example, did she allow a patient to use her nickname "Hattie."

Dada believed in the healing and comforting powers of her strong religious faith and felt the calling to work within her power to counter the morally degrading influences of military life. She points out in her reminiscences a number of cases where she assisted her patients in renewing their faith in God. She supported

---

10. Documents in support of Dada's pension submitted to the 51st Congress found in Record Group 46, Legislative Branch, Sen. 51 A - E1, Box 10, National Archives, Washington, D.C.: Bruce, *Onondaga's Centennial*, Vol. II, Part III, "Family Sketches," p. 15.

the work of hospital chaplains and used her contacts with upstate New York churches to enlist their aid for her work. While at Aquia Landing for example, her sister Elizabeth, on Harriet's behalf, asked the children of the Homer Congregational Church to make soldier "comfort bags" and send them on to Dada with their personal notes for distribution to the sick. In her return thank you letter, Harriet told the children that many of the soldiers had acquired the bad habits of smoking and drinking whiskey in order to relieve their loneliness. "If any of you have brothers in the army," she wrote, "I hope you will send them so many letters and papers that they will have no such excuses."[11]

Although Dada traveled extensively with the army, only once, during Thomas "Stonewall" Jackson's Shenandoah Valley Campaign of 1862, did she find herself caught up in the fighting. On May 22, she rode with three other nurses in an ambulance from Winchester to Strasburg to care for the sick at a hospital under the protection of troops from Major General Nathaniel P. Banks' Union command. Jackson's men struck the next day from the south and drove Banks' men north to the Potomac River, leaving Dada and a number of other nurses in enemy hands at Winchester. The Confederates abandoned Winchester on May 31 and marched back south up the valley through Strasburg on June 1, 1862. Union troops recaptured Winchester soon after and rescued the nurses.

About 1890, Dada's many friends and supporters successfully promoted a bill in Congress to provide her with a military pension. At that time many former patients submitted affidavits in her behalf.[12] The following are excerpts from some of these testimonials praising her exceptional service as a nurse and her devotion to duty.

> I knew Miss Dada as the good nurse and soldier's friend. ...with sleeves rolled up and towel in hand she would meet the wounded comrade fresh from the battle field, take charge of loving messages from the dying, and assist in Christian services for those desiring them.
> H. G. Potter
> Sergeant, Company A,
> 74th Indiana Infantry

---

11. Handwritten copy of letter found in Dada genealogical file, Cortland County Historical Society, Cortland, New York.
12. Affidavits found in Record Group 46, Legislative Branch, Sen 51A - E1, Box 10.

There was not an hour in the day...when she was not present with cheerful, pleasant mien, encouraging the sick and wounded, soothing the distressed, and whispering words of comfort to the dying. [The boys appreciated] the sight of her bright, intelligent, modest, loving face as she passed from cot-to-cot on her angelic mission....

> Francis W. Drake
> Sergeant, Company L,
> 1st Minnesota Heavy Artillery

Miss Dada was a very popular nurse. She was very kind, very efficient, very industrious, and intelligent, and done all for the...sick soldier that a good, kind, generous, patriotic women could do....

> J. Mercer
> Captain, Company E,
> 147th Pennsylvania Infantry

The doctors...said I could not live and I was indifferent whether I lived or died, and she...bid me live. To her, more than to all else, I owe the life and strength and happiness which I now enjoy. [...] What she did for me she did for hundreds of others as helpless and hopeless. [...] She did for us all that a sister, wife or mother could do.

> William H. Bright
> Company C,
> 22nd Wisconsin Infantry

In recognition of her service to her patients in the 12th Army Corps, a number of corps medical officers on April 2, 1865 awarded her a special corps badge. The citation identified the gift "as a memento of our respect for your untiring devotion to the cause you so nobly espoused during the dark days of our Country's History." In her last article for the *National Tribune,* Dada provides a description of the badge and indicates that she received it on May 9, 1865.

In 1868 Dada obtained a degree from the New York Medical College for Women in New York City[13] and a few months later became a homeopathic physician in Syracuse, New York, specializing in diseases of women and children. She married Reverend Peter Walter Emens in December 1873.[14] She died in Syracuse on September 1, 1909 and was buried in Oakwood Cemetery under a small stone identified only by her initials. The Harriet Dada Emens Tent 63, Daughters of Union Veterans of the Civil War in Cortland County, was named in her honor.[15]

*Dada's grave in Oakwood Cemetery, Syracuse, NY.*

The following is an exact reproduction of Dada's ten articles published in the weekly *National Tribune* newspaper running consecutively from February 7, 1884 through the April 10 issue. I would like to thank the following individuals for assisting me in doing research for the accompanying notes: Mr. Ben Ritter, Winchester, Virginia; Mike Musick, National Archives, Washington, D.C.; Mr. Jim Ogden, Chickamauga and Chattanooga National Military Park; Scott Hartwig, Gettysburg National Military Park; Melinda Day, Harpers Ferry National Historical Park; Anita Wright, Cortland County Historical Society, Cortland, New York; Rebekah A. Ambrose, Onondaga Historical Association, Syracuse, New York; and Lynda L. Sudlow, North Yarmouth, Maine.

---

13. The New York Medical College and Hospital for women was a homeopathic institution established by Clemence Sophia Lozier (1813-1888) in April 1863. The college was the first women's school of medicine in the state. It later merged with the New York Homeopathic Medical College. See Lozier sketch in *Notable American Women, 1607-1950*, ed. by Edward T. James (Cambridge, Massachusetts, and London, England: The Belknap Press of Harvard University Press, 1971), Vol. II, pp. 440-3.
14. Eileen F. Conklin, *Women at Gettysburg, 1863* (Gettysburg: Thomas Publications, 1993), p. 272; Bruce, *Onondaga's Centennial*, Vol. II, Part III, "Family Sketches," p. 16. Emens, a widower with three children, was born 1831 in Romulus, Seneca Co. He graduated from Union College, and became a physician and a minister in the Presbyterian Church.
15. Dada genealogical file, Cortland County Historical Society, Cortland, New York.

# I.

In June, 1861, it was my privilege to be numbered with those selected by the Ladies-Central Association of Relief to attend the surgical practice in the New York city hospitals, that we might be the better prepared to take our places as nurses in the army hospitals which were in anticipation. Daily, for six weeks, I visited the different wards, witnessed the operations, learned the mysteries of bandaging, etc.

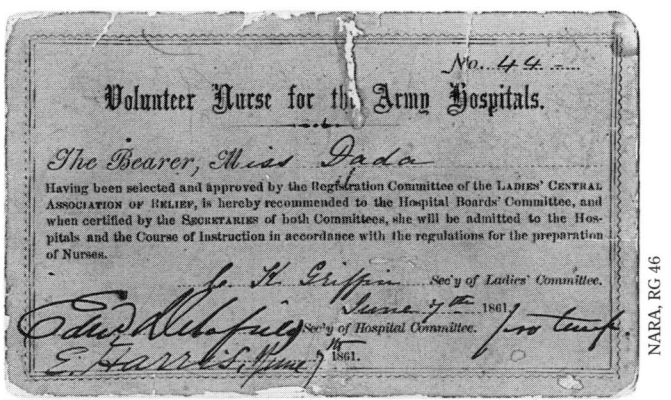

Many remember the battle-cry, "On to Richmond," which filled the daily papers of July, 1861. The programme was: "One decisive battle," then Richmond would be ours, and the Confederate congress captured. Sharing the general feeling, I was anxious to do my part in the "short struggle" in the way of caring for the sick and the wounded. Little did I then think that my services would be needed till the last of September, 1865.

On the morning of July 22, 1861, I read with a mingled feeling of pain and pleasure the following:

> Room 21, 1st Hall.
> 
> Will Miss Dada call as soon as possible at the Cooper Institute this afternoon and bring Miss Hall, if she knows her address?
> 
> E. [Elizabeth] Blackwell

The pain felt was the realization of the long-dreaded fact that the sword had been unsheathed, the war had actually begun, and that fathers, husbands and brothers were already dead, dying and wounded on the battlefield, whom mothers, wives and sisters could not reach; and the pleasure was the prospect of soon being amid those busy scenes, binding up the wounds and doing with my might all that could be done for the comfort of our country's defenders. Rumors were rife. Some said: "We have been beaten at Bull Run." Others said: "No; for we have an army of such magnitude." Miss Hall — who is now Mrs. Susan Hall Barry, of San Francisco, Cal. — and I were soon at Cooper Institute, where we were instructed to be at the Jersey City ferry and take the 6 o'clock p.m. train for Washington and report to Miss [Dorothea] Dix. At the appointed time we were on the way to the seat of war. Tuesday morning, on reaching Washington, we found all excitement. Reporting to Miss Dix, the only question she asked was: "Are you ready to work?" Answering in the affirmative, she added: "You are needed in Alexandria."

## EN ROUTE TO ALEXANDRIA

Time passed slowly, and we could hardly wait till the afternoon, when, seated in a hack, we started for Alexandria. Our progress was slow. The streets were filled with soldiers, worn out and hungry, straggling in from the field of battle. On the Long Bridge we were obliged to stop and allow retreating army wagons to pass. Seeing a newly-equipped regiment marching through the streets of a northern city was one thing, and that same regiment subsequently marching in disorder and confusion, their uniforms soiled with dust and they chagrined with retreating, was quite another thing. Across the bridge, in some little cabins by the roadside, we first saw the wounded, to whom we could only give a word of cheer and pass on.

We rode through the ponderous gates of Fort Runyon, in the direction of Alexandria. Frequently we met officers, of whom we inquired if there was any danger of the approach of the enemy; if the roads were safe, etc. The town we reached in safety. We stopped in front of a dark stone building on Washington street, which was formerly a seminary, but now a hospital filled with the wounded.[16] At the door we were rather unceremoniously stopped by a guard, who informed us we could not enter. Soon, however, Dr. [Henry Lawrence] Sheldon, the surgeon in charge, made his appearance, who admitted us and accepted our services, saying,

---

16. This apparently was "Brimstone Castle" or Benjamin Hallowell's Alexandria Boarding School on North Washington Street in Alexandria, Virginia. However, an extant photograph of the old building (no longing standing) shows it as being made of brick.

as he led the way to the rooms where were the wounded: "Here are the men needing such care as women can bestow — a kind word, a drink of water, their wounds bathed; anything for their comfort will be acceptable." We found some on beds, others on mattresses on the floors. Many were still covered with the dust of the retreat, because wounded arms could not wash faces and wounded legs could not move about; so we were soon at work.

## PLENTY OF WORK

Those who entered hospitals at a later day have no idea of the unsettled state of things that we found. At this time no soldiers were detailed for nurses, and were not till in November, so we had wounds to dress with water every hour, faces, hands, and feet to wash, beds to arrange, food and water to distribute, medicines to give, and, in fact, everything to do for the sick and the wounded, with no help except that of a contraband, who assisted about the various wards, and who, soon becoming weary of steady employment, would leave; when another one would be found, who in turn would take his departure. Thus for weeks, day and night, we were kept constantly busy.

At first the food was pretty poor, but it could not be helped. The soldiers would get so tired of bread, butter, and tea for supper, and bread and coffee for breakfast! This was all they had, and we had just the same. Afterwards, the good people of the North, through the Sanitary Commission and other agencies, sent us some jellies, fruits, &c., which added greatly to the comfort of the soldiers.

There was no chaplain in our hospital. Those connected with the regiments about would sometimes come in and visit the wards. None of the pastors of the churches in town ever came to visit the sick and wounded, except one Roman Catholic priest. Neither did the white people come in, but many good Christian colored people often came and brought something good for the soldiers, saying as they did so, "I pray for you every day." One colored family, who had the care of a large house and gardens near by, supplied us with bouquets of beautiful flowers.

## THE FIRST DEATH

In the wards assigned to Miss Hall and myself none of the wounded died till August 12th. Amos Schofield [sic],[17] of the 1st Minnesota, who had been wounded through the neck, the ball coming out of his mouth and knocking out several teeth, was the first. The earliest entry in his diary was Tuesday, April 23, 1861: "I left home and friends to-day to enlist in the company from Goodhue county, to serve my country, to fight for God and liberty." He did his work well. He suffered patiently, and, at last, bled to death. Towards the last his wound would not allow him to speak, but he wrote on a piece of paper, "Write to my mother that I die happy in Christ."

Weeks and months passed on. Changes were taking place all the time. The hospital was kept full. When one left, whether as convalescent or by death, another took his place. Our hospital bore a good name. According to the number of patients we had the fewest deaths of any in the district. More died from disease than from wounds, and still, of a number of severe cases of typhoid fever in my ward in December and January, only one died.

One evening in September I was passing through the ward above mine for a few moments, when a young Maine soldier, suffering from diphtheria, looked up and asked in a whisper: "Can't you get some one to come and fan me?" I sat down and fanned him for a while, and as I was leaving to give some medicine to one in my own ward, he said: "Tell doctor to come quick, for I can scarcely breathe." I did as he requested, and asked the doctor if he could live? "No," he replied; "and you must go sit by his side, fan him, and tell him his situation. He ought to know it, but I can't tell him." I never knew till then the difficulty of telling one that the sands of life were nearly run — that he must die. On my return I took a rose, full bloom, and handed it to him. He looked a pleasant "thank you." Gradually I approached the subject. Poor boy! Only nineteen; he felt he must go home and see his friends. A comrade come[sic] from the regiment to spend the night with him. This cheered him. In the night I returned to his bed-side and spent an hour with him. He became conscious that he could not live. He asked: "What shall I do to be saved?" I pointed him to the Lamb of God. He wanted me to pray with him, which I did. He also prayed. A solemn hour! Towards morning I again was beside him. On asking him if his trust was in the Saviour? "yes," was his reply. Soon he became restless, and at 6 a.m. he was dead. Miss Hall and I prepared his body for the grave, and at 6 in the evening "Charlie," of the 5th Maine, was borne to his last resting place. His full name I know not.[18]

---

17. Amos G. Scofield, Company F, 1st Minnesota Infantry.
18. Probably Private Charles W. Bucknell, Company H, 5th Maine Infantry who died 17 September 1861. Service Records indicate that he died in the hospital at Alexandria.

## II.

In December a new hospital was opened in Alexandria.[19] A rumor went out that "no women or niggers were to be employed in it." Everything needed was to be furnished, and the sick soldiers were to be left to the care of men detailed from the regiment. However, on opening the hospital ladies were admitted as nurses. It is well known that from the first there was opposition to having female nurses in the hospitals. Surgeon-General [Clement A.] Finley was always opposed to them, and many others under him felt the same. This subjected us to more or less annoyance. One of the surgeons in this new hospital said to one of the ladies: "A lady ceases to be a lady when she becomes a nurse." Such unpleasant expressions fell with but little weight upon our ears; for we knew that our days and nights of care, watching and anxiety over the sick and wounded were appreciated by thousands of their friends at home. The many letters we received from the friends of those for whom we cared, so full of thanks, more than compensated for the unkind words and sneers.

### A DIABOLICAL PLOT

During the month of January, 1862, the Confederates formed a plot to blow up Mansion House hospital. The powder was laid to connect in the cellar, but discovered in time to prevent the consummation of the diabolical plan. Alexandria was full of rebel citizens at that time.[20]

On the 6th of March a new hospital was opened in Wolf[e] street, consisting of two elegant private residences, surrounded with nice yards.[21] One had eighty-two and the other sixty-one beds. Miss Hall was assigned to one building and I to the other. They were both filled with those having the measles, mostly from the 5th Michigan.

---

19. The Mansion House Hospital on the corner of Fairfax and Cameron Streets.
20. For the newspaper description of this event that probably provided Dada her information see "the Mansion House Affair," *The Local News*, Alexandria, Va., 10 January 1862. Found on microfilm in the Lloyd House public library, Alexandria, Va.
21. See photograph of Wolfe street buildings. One of the buildings still stands.

Alexandria Library, Special Collections

*Wolfe Street hospital, Alexandria, Va.*

On the 20th of this month I received a telegram from my brother [Samuel Newell Dada], which read: "Father is not expected to live. Come home." Permission was given me, and soon arrangements were made, and I was on my way North. Before reaching home my father had fallen asleep, and I found nothing but the lifeless form of him who had always welcomed me with a father's love. But there was great comfort in the knowledge that he had passed away in his own quiet home, where loving hands had ministered to his wants.

I had been home but one week, when news came that a battle had been fought at Winchester, Va. I started back at once to the scene.[22]

On reaching Washington I learned arrangements had been made for Miss Hall and myself to go to Winchester, Va. I only had time to go to Alexandria and call on my old friends at Wolf[e]-street hospital. I found all improving, but not well pleased at our leaving; yet consenting, as they knew the wounded needed our care.

From Washington we took cars for Harper's [sic] Ferry. Stopping at Sandy Hook, on the Maryland side of the river, we waited three hours for the train to make up for Winchester. On attempting to get our trunks on board, we were told that no civilians would be allowed to go, as the Government had taken the cars to transport stores, &c., and only one car of soldiers would be sent out. Informing them of our mission, we were permitted to enter the

---

22. Dada refers to the Battle of Kernstown, Virginia, fought March 23, 1862.

car. We were five hours in going thirty miles, reaching Winchester about 9 o'clock in the evening.

We were directed to, and spent the night with, a Union family by the name of Jackson.[23] The husband had been taken away as prisoner by General Stonewall Jackson, and had not been heard from in several weeks.

Although two weeks had passed since the battle, we found everything very much unsettled in the Union Hotel hospital.[24] Nothing was ready for the comfort of the wounded as they were brought in from the battlefield. On Monday, after the battle, thirty-seven had died in this hospital. For days they laid on the floor. The Confederate women brought in things for their wounded, but passed ours by, till the surgeon told them they should not enter the hospital if they continued doing so. The Union people, both white and colored, daily brought food from their own homes and distributed to all alike.

In the ward to which I was assigned were eight who had been severely wounded, and the nurses had been bathing all their wounds from one basin of water, which set on a table in the center of the room, which had once been the large dining-room of the hotel. Why the surgeon had not instructed them to do differently, I never knew.

On April 10, 1862, the patients were removed to more comfortable quarters in Seminary hospital;[25] but some of them were too low to be moved with safety, especially Sergeant Charles Kneggs and Alexander Retan, of the 14th Indiana, also Peter Miller; all of whom subsequently died. There was no necessity for moving them, but "the order" was imperative. The surgeon refused to have any female nurses in that hospital, which order brought sorrow to the sick and wounded, as well as to ourselves, for we had willing hands and hearts, and saw enough to do for the comfort of those to whom we had come to minister. At the same time the medical authorities were not willing to have us leave town, but said, "Await further orders."

---

23. Joseph S. and Mary D. Jackson. Their stone house stands at 35 West Piccadilly Street in Winchester.
24. The Union Hotel, at the northeast corner of what are today Cameron Street and Fairfax Lane, collapsed in December of 1864. Cameron Street was named Market Street at the time of the Civil War.
25. This building, also known as the Valley Female Institute and the York Hospital, is located at 112 South Cameron Street. Records show the surgeon in charge at Winchester at this time to be James D. Robison. "Registers of Army Hospitals and their Staffs," Record group 112, Entry 219, National Archives, Washington, D.C.

C.[sic][26]H. Worcester, of the 7th Ohio, a young man greatly beloved by his company, died in the Union Hotel hospital. He remarked to his tent-mate, just before entering the battle, that if any of them should fall in battle, the "Faithful Sentinel" should be sung by those who remained. The words were peculiarly applicable to him, especially the third verse.

> "He wept not himself, that his warfare was done,
> The battle was fought and the victory won;
> But he whispered to those whom his heart loved most,
> Tell my brethren for me, that I died at my post."

Some lives seemed to have been needlessly sacrificed. We were told that surgeons were known to stop and dispute as to which of them should perform the operation, and then, after the amputation, instead of attending to the sufferer, they would play with the dismembered hand, foot or limb. Such surgeons should have been summarily discharged. Fortunately they were in the minority; for many were true and noble gentlemen, and very skillful.

On the 16th of April, not being allowed to care for the wounded in the hospitals, we visited the battlefield. We saw the orchard where our boys threw off their blankets and knapsacks before going into action. We passed on to where they marched to victory and many of them to death. The hill where the artillery was placed was pointed out to us, and where the flank movement to the right was made. The trees in the woods showed marks of the shot and shell. These woods were at the head of the famous stone wall behind which so many Confederates fell. We passed over the ground, which had been contested inch by inch. I picked up a ball near where one of the 1st Virginia (Union) fell. His foot and stocking were still there, and the blood on the ground showed where he had lain. We crossed over the stone wall, where, within a short distance, seventy-two Confederates were found dead, and thence to the brow of the hill, where the Confederates, concealed from our boys, poured a volley upon them as they came up. Fortunately their aim was two [sic] high. Then followed close fighting. The colonel of the 84th Pennsylvania [Col. William Gray Murray] fell there. His last words were: "Boys, I am no longer your colonel." Near by, the brave 14th Indiana marched on. Alexander Retan, whose death I mentioned above, bore the regimental colors, and one next to him the stars and stripes. The bearer of the

---

26. Orlando H. Worcester, Company C, 7th Ohio Infantry.

stars and stripes fell wounded. He called for some one to take them. Just as Retan grasped the standard a ball pierced his body and he fell, too. A third one took it, and he, also, was shot with a bullet from a Confederate gun. The last two died of their wounds, while the first recovered. We noticed a small enclosure where eighty-four Confederates were said to have been buried in a trench. On some of the head-boards of the buried dead the names were given; of others, simply the word "Unknown."

The medical directors, on April 20, sent for Miss Hall and the writer, and asked us to attend to some who were sick in the courthouse and in a loft over a vacated store. We found they needed our care. The loft consisted of four rooms, miserable, dark, unpleasant, over-run with rats. The counters were used for tables for the convalescents, but there were no suitable rooms or conveniences for taking care of the sick. Soon after I went there Richard Lee Henry, of the lst Virginia (Union) [cavalry], died.

While there, word came to me one day that Peter Miller, whose name I have above mentioned, could not live over twenty-four hours. He was mortally wounded. The ball had broken the bone of the upper arm and entered his side, passing through his lung and out at his back. When I first reached Winchester and entered the ward, two weeks after the battle, the blood and dirt had not been cleaned from his arm and hand; nor had his face been washed or his hair combed. On hearing that he was worse I immediately went to see him. The old surgeon, whom I met at the door, told me there was no chance for Peter to live, adding: "You must not tell him." I was very sorry to receive such an order, for I wanted to know his feelings in view of death. His bright black eyes had an unnatural lustre that afternoon. He talked cheerfully with me as usual; said he was doing finely, and wanted me to write a letter for him. I then talked with him about Christ and the necessary preparation for another world. Finishing my conversation, I shook hands with him, saying: "I will come to see you to-morrow." The next day, on going there, he had been dead about an hour. When he knew he was dying he asked: "Why did you not tell me?" He was an orphan, and long will he be remembered by those who took care of him.

In time, the hospital was moved from the loft to the Odd Fellows' hall,[27] where, in a more commodious room, the sick improved

---

27. The Odd Fellows Hall no longer stands at its 1 South Cameron Street location.

much faster. Miss [Mary] Duncan, from Pittsburgh, Pa., prepared the diet for the sick, and she cooked everything just right; her services were invaluable.

In the afternoon of May 21, the post surgeon called and said Miss Hall and I must go the next day to Strasburg, sixteen miles farther south, towards the front, to take care of many who were there sick, and that an ambulance would call for us at 8 o'clock in the morning.

# III.

On the morning of May 22, 1862, the ambulance called for Miss Hall, two other ladies, and myself, and took us to Strasburg. There we found Mrs. [Abby H.] Gibbons and her daughter [Sarah H. (Emerson)], from New York city, preparing delicacies for the sick, and they gladly welcomed us. At Winchester they had performed a similar service. Here at Strasburg were some eight hundred sick. One meeting-house was filled with them, and the rest were in tents. The day after our arrival Miss Hall was assigned to the church and I to the tents, and we forthwith commenced our work.[28]

That evening we saw troops going out in great haste on the Front Royal road. General [Nathaniel P.] Banks' headquarters were in town: and regiments were stationed on all sides. Our rooms were in a small house, a short distance from the hospital. In the night we were awakened by a noise in the streets. They were calling up soldiers, telling them to get ready to skedaddle. Ere long a loud rap was heard at our door, and a man from the hospital directed us to pack our things in a hurry, as we were surrounded by the enemy, and an ambulance would soon call for us. Being told to leave our trunks behind, we started as soon as the ambulance came, without our baggage. While yet in town an officer met us, and, on learning we had not taken our baggage with us, informed us that we had better return for it, and he would send another ambulance for us. We returned, found the house with difficulty, and waited a long hour for the ambulance, which, when it came, had a colored man for a driver, his wife accompanying him. It was about 4 o'clock when we started. General confusion reigned! All were eager to reach a place of safety. It was a sorrowful sight: the long wagon train, reaching as far as the eye could see; the streets filled with soldiers — some just from the hospital, — and ambulances loaded with the sick. A retreat cannot be described. One must be in it in order to know what it is. As opportunity afforded, we hurried past teams in advance of us, till at last we got ahead of the train and hastening on to Winchester, reached there about 11 a.m. We found Winchester all excitement. The

---

28. The church was most likely the brick Strasburg Presbyterian Church.

Confederates were expecting Stonewall Jackson there to take tea with them that evening, and the women of the town were hurrying to and fro in the streets, making due preparations for his reception. Towards evening the ambulances arrived, bringing their precious freight of sick to the hospitals. The Union Hotel was soon filled, as also the lower room of the court-house. Some died just as they were taken from the ambulances; others were in a dying condition, and in their delerium[sic] thought the rebels were trying to get them. Soon Dr. [John B.] Coover arrived and expressed his delight at finding us. An ambulance had been captured and he had been fearful that it was ours.

## A MEMORABLE NIGHT

In the evening the wounded began to come in from the rear, which had been attacked. About 9 o'clock I accompanied Miss Hall, who was completely worn out, to the Union Hotel, some of the 10th Maine [Infantry] guarding us through the town. All night the wounded were being brought in, and most of the time no surgeon was there. What beds we had were spread on the floor; when they were occupied we used blankets, and soon the floor was covered. Some were severely wounded and in great pain. We dressed their wounds as well as we could. Sergeant [Silas M.] Atwood, of the 5th New York cavalry, wounded in the leg, had been brought several miles on horse back, and was completely exhausted. He only lived a few days.

With daylight, Sunday morning, came action. Cavalry, with sabers drawn, rode through the town to join General Banks, who the night before had made a stand about a mile out. More wounded were being brought in. Breakfast was to be prepared for all, and no rations had been drawn. Coffee, bread and gruel was all we had for them. Rumors were afloat that the town would be burned rather than it should fall into the enemy's hands, and on seeing fires near the depot we began to think it might be so. Then came word that Banks had given an order to retreat. Our troops came pouring through the town, followed by the Confederates, shouting, firing guns, and causing a confusion which cannot be described. In the hospital, paleness was on every countenance and anxiety in every eye; for we had heard that the sick and wounded had been bayoneted at Front Royal the day before. Even then some were dying. One whom I remember as seeing at Strasburg very sick, in the midst of all this confusion breathed his last. His name was Matthias Patricks,[29] from or near Lockport, New York. I do not know that his friends ever learned his fate.

As soon as the Confederates had secured possession of the town a guard was placed at our door — not, however, till several Confederate balls had come flying through the hospital, wounding one of the nurses and a little colored boy who was near the door. The seven ladies, who composed the force of nurses in the different hospitals, had decided, the day before, to remain at their posts, even if the town fell into the hands of the enemy; for then they would be there to take care of the sick and wounded. Miss Duncan and I were at the court-house, and Miss Hall at the Union Hotel. More thankful soldiers I never saw than were the wounded that day and the days following, to find Northern loyal ladies ready to do all in their power for them. It must be remembered that but few sanitary stores had reached Winchester, except such as private charity brought. Of the Christian Commission we had not as yet heard. Therefore, we had few comforts for the wounded.

## UNDER CONFEDERATE RULE

All day the Confederates were bringing in our men as prisoners and placing them in the court-house yard, and by evening it was full. Many a Confederate rode into town with his horse loaded with clothing, which had been thrown away by our fleeing soldiers, or had been stripped from the dead. The bodies of several Union men, who had been shot in the streets, were brought into the hall of the court-house and lay there two or three days.

Monday morning we had nothing but coffee and gruel for breakfast for the patients, but there was not a word of complaint. In the forenoon Miss Duncan went to the Confederate authorities and informed them of the fact, and they immediately sent us some bread. Vegetables and meat could not be procured. As several of our surgeons had been taken prisoners, however, the wounded had all the surgical attention they needed.

In two or three days all our sick and wounded in the three hospitals were, by orders of the Confederates, crowded into the Union Hotel, and the vacated buildings, with all their stores, were taken by the Confederates for their own wounded. Aside from being

---

29. Probably Marcellus E. Patrick(s), 28th New York Infantry.

overcrowded we fared very well. Our prisoners were not well treated, however, by the rebels, which grated on our feelings.

In a few days the Confederate troops returned from the North, and turned their steps towards the South, taking many prisoners with them. Before leaving they paroled all who were in the hospital, May 31, 1862, leaving enough to guard us, with an order for all to remain in the hospital, and notified us that if any of us were seen in the streets we would be shot. The first Union troops that made their appearance after the retirement of the Confederates came from the South. They were cavalry, and the sight of their blue uniforms brought much joy to us.

## GENERAL SIGEL'S VISIT

On the 14th of June General [Franz] Sigel visited the hospital, dressed in citizen's clothes, and accompanied by a Union lady, who had often been there before. He was stopped at the door by the guard, but one of the nurses said it was "all right," and the general remarked: "I like to see the guard do his duty." The general had in his hand a tumbler of jelly, and had he been recognized he would have been received with more demonstration. The day following, General Banks and staff visited the hospital — the second time after his return from his retreat into Maryland. He spoke with each patient in my ward, remarking that they looked more comfortable than when he was last there.

About the lst of July many of the patients were removed from this hospital to Academy hospital,[30] a little out of town, which was a more healthy location, and on the 8th of that month Miss Hall and I were ordered there. We found some Confederates who had been left to act as nurses. The Confederate wounded were from Louisiana and North Carolina regiments. One of them remarked one day: "If Jefferson Davis had fought and suffered as I have, he would be sick of it." They were greatly surprised at being so kindly treated in the hospital, and one of them remarked to me: "If I could only let my wife know how comfortably I am cared for, I should be very glad; because the Confederates have told the people that the Yankees killed all their prisoners." Many of them learned there for the first time that the North was fighting from very different principles and motives than they had been taught to believe.

---

30. The Winchester Academy, a large brick and stone building, stood west of town. The school did not survive the war.

About the 12th of July the hospitals in town were broken up and the wounded moved to Harper's Ferry. The journey was made in boxcars, and we were nine hours going thirty miles, reaching the ferry at midnight. In the morning (Sunday) the patients were taken up the hill in ambulances to the hospital, which was beautifully located in one of the most romantic places I ever saw.[31] Two other ladies went from Winchester with Miss Hall and myself — a Miss [Mary J.] Welch and another, whose name I do not recall. We occupied a little house by ourselves, near the patients, who were in houses and tents.

On the 25th of July Miss Hall and I were ordered to report to Washington. As the other two ladies had left, both of us could not be spared — so Miss Hall went without me. Mrs. [Abba A.] Goddard, M. D., from Maine, had charge of the diet kitchen. She had brought many supplies with her from Maine. I was busy dressing wounds, and the patients were by this time doing very well.

---

31. The Clayton General Hospital consisted primarily of tents and two large residences associated with the Harpers Ferry Armory; the paymaster's quarters (Lockwood House) and the superintendent's quarters. Both houses survive and are preserved by the National Park Service (Harpers Ferry National Historical Park). The paymaster's house where many of the patients were kept has been restored by the park to its Civil War appearance.

Harpers Ferry National Historical Park

*Lockwood House, part of the hospital at Harpers Ferry.*

## AT THE CAPITAL AGAIN

About the 15th of August, learning that the hospital was soon to be broken up, I went to Washington, and soon after reaching there was assigned to Ward G, Armory Square hospital, in which was several cases of typhoid fever. There I was kept very busy both day and night. Many of the wounded from the second battle of Bull Run were brought directly to this hospital. Mrs. [Harriet J.] Wright from Saco, Maine, did valuable service in the same ward; and we, as well as the wounded, were daily cheered by the visits of Mrs. Charles Hendley of Washington, who brought many a delicacy to the suffering. A large number of the wounded died. I remember the names of few of them. Edwin Reed,[32] of Gardiner, Maine, whose arm had been amputated, was at first expected to live; but bad symptoms soon appeared, and we saw he could not recover. He was very grateful for all that was done for him, and asked why he, a stranger, should receive such kindness? He desired me to pray for him and to be by his side as much as possible. Just before he died I asked him if he knew me; for he was delirious much of the time. Summoning all the strength he could he murmured "Hattie," — a liberty I had allowed him, because he had a sister of that name, and my other name was so hard for him to remember. When he died, Mrs. Hendley, who also had become very much interested in him, wrote to his parents, informing them of their son's death. His name was ever mentioned with tenderness, for he was one of the noblest boys who fell in defending his country.

Another patient was wounded in the foot, and dangerous symptoms soon manifested themselves. When it was seen that he could not recover, I informed him of the fact, in answer to his inquiry. At first he seemed somewhat startled, but afterwards became calm. The chaplain conversed and prayed with him several times. On the morning of the day he died, I handed a piece of paper and pencil to him, asking him to write a "good-bye" to his mother. He had often spoken of her very tenderly, and said that she was praying for him, &c. Taking the pencil he wrote:

> Dear father, mother, and brothers, farewell! I rest in the arms of my dear Saviour.
> 
> J. Harbolt

---

32. Company C, 1st Maine Cavalry.

A few days after, an elderly gentleman came to our ward and inquired if any of the 20th Indiana were there. He was told that Jonathan Harbolt had been one of the inmates, but had died. He was the boy's father, who had heard of his son's sickness, and had come on to see him. His heart was nearly broken. He did not take his son's body home, thinking no place so appropriate for a soldier's grave as the capital of the country in the defense of which he had lost his life. A few days after his death came a commission, promoting him to be 2d lieutenant for his bravery at Fair Oaks. But it came too late; he was already promoted above all confusion and strife.[33]

---

33. Records show Jonathan Harbolt, 2nd Lieutenant, Co. K, 20th Indiana Infantry as being buried at Arlington National Cemetery.

## IV.

In November, 1862, Miss Hall, who for several weeks had been taking care of the wounded at Antietam, came to Washington for hospital stores, and as my experience at Armory Square hospital made me anxious to get away from so much "red tape" and go where the real comfort of the sick and the wounded was the chief concern of those in charge of them, it was decided that I should return with Miss Hall as far as Harper's Ferry. We reached there the 8th of November, and I learned that a new 12th army corps hospital was to be opened that evening. Miss Duncan had preceded me. The building to be occupied was on the bank of the Shenandoah River. It was a large five-story structure, and had formerly been a factory.[34]

The fourth story was the first to be filled with the sick. There were iron cots, straw beds, and good new blankets, but pillows, sheets and even stoves we did not have for some days, because they could not be obtained. We were obliged to heat bricks and carry them up to those who could not otherwise keep warm.

Some of the patients were so covered with vermin that their clothes had to be destroyed. Many of the regiments had had no opportunity to draw clothing since a date prior to Pope's retreat, and with disease and vermin preying upon them all those long months, many were quite reduced to skeletons. The surgeon ordered the heads of several to be shaven, and I made woolen caps for them. One looked so poor and haggard that I thought he must be an old man, but I found him to be a boy only eighteen years of age. He was so emaciated that his cheek-bones had pierced the skin, and his voice sounded sepulchral. He lived but a week. In many cases I could tell how long they had been sick by the color of their hands and faces. On entering the ward with a basin of water and towel many hands would beckon me to come to them, calling out: "Lady, come here;" or, "Come here; I want a woman to take care of me when I'm sick." Every morning I found vacant beds. The occupants had passed beyond the care of any one.

Dr. [H. Earnest] Goodman was in charge of the hospital, and he saw in a short time that every comfort and convenience the Government could furnish was provided. I have often thought

---

34. The Cotton Factory Hospital building (1848–1936) was located on Virginius Island. Only a part of the foundation is visible today.

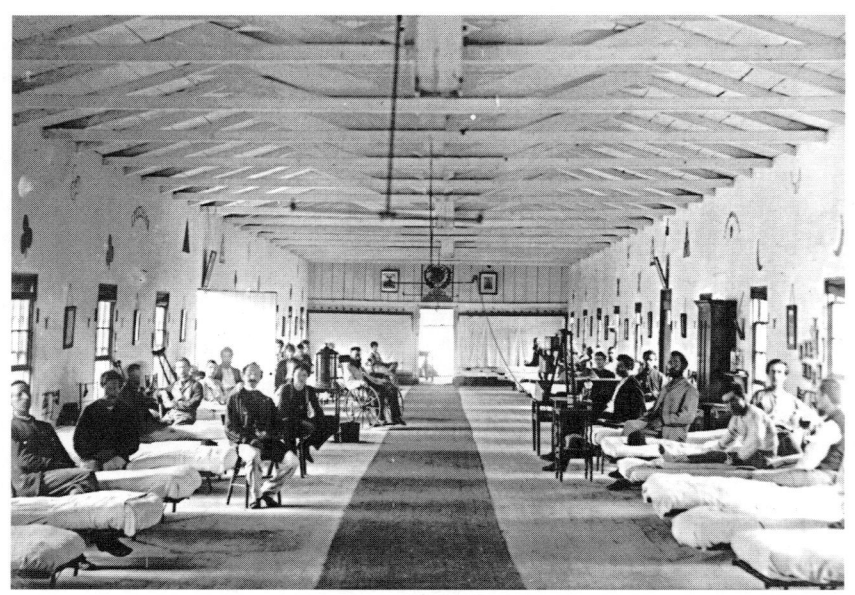

Library of Congress

*Ward K, Armory Square hospital.*

Harpers Ferry National Historical Park

*Cotton Factory hospital, Harpers Ferry.*
*Factory is shown as tall structure with cupola along river.*

that if the other surgeons in charge of hospitals had had the interest of those under their care as much at heart as did Dr. Goodman, there would have been far less need of Sanitary and Christian Commissions. It was evident that the Government did furnish liberally when proper requisitions were made. In many cases, unfortunately, too little interest was taken by those in charge of the hospitals.

About the 18th of November Miss Hall returned from Antietam and was assigned to duty in the ward with me, and in December, Misses [Annie] Bell, [Sallie E.] Dysart and [Elizabeth A.] Tuttle joined us, for at that time every floor was filled with very sick patients. And so months passed, each day being filled with cares and anxieties from early in the morning till late at night.

## SENT TO THE FRONT AGAIN

After the battle near Acquia [Aquia][35] Creek, Dr. Goodman, who had been ordered to the front, telegraphed for Mrs. [sic] Duncan, Miss Hall, and myself to come on immediately. Owing, however, to unaccountable and red-tape delays in getting passes in Washington, it was not till the 22d of May that we reached the 12th army corps hospital, in which we found many severely wounded. I was assigned to duty in the 2d division. In one tent I found Ed. [Edmund M] Bullen, of the 2d Massachusetts, who just one year before had been a faithful nurse in the hospital at Winchester, seriously wounded through the left lung, and very weak. He was among those who, in the cold and rain, had lain on the battlefield for twelve days. It seemed impossible for him to recover; but after the war closed I wrote to his wife for information concerning him, and received an answer in his own handwriting, informing me of his recovery. He was then working at his trade.

One Sunday morning, about the middle of June, orders were received at our hospital to move all the wounded on transports to Washington, as the army had moved and was following Lee into Pennsylvania. I waited in Washington till I heard of the battle of Gettysburg, and then started for the field, reaching the town, which I found in great confusion, on the evening of July 6th. It was with difficulty that I found a place in which to spend the night. Early in the morning I inquired at the courthouse hospital of the lst army

---

35. Dada here refers to the Battle of Chancellorsville, May 1–4. 1863.

corps for news of the 147th New York, which regiment was in the first day's fight. I learned that Lieut. Schenck from my home in Oswego county, N.Y., had been wounded and was in a hotel near by. On entering the room where he was, he exclaimed, "Why, Hattie Dada, I did not expect to see you here." When I saw his wound, my heart sank within me, for I knew he could not live. In a few days his father and sister came; but with all their care he steadily failed, and before a month had passed was numbered with the dead. He said to me, "I should have been ashamed to have remained at home and felt that others were sacrificing their lives for me." Fulton never sent out a braver, truer-hearted soldier than Lieutenant Wm. Schenck.

After seeing that Lieutenant Schenck had a good attendant from his own company, I looked for a 12th army corps hospital ambulance, and soon found one filled with goods from the Sanitary Commission, which was ahead of the Government in getting supplies to the wounded at Gettysburg.

## IN A GETTYSBURG HOSPITAL

We passed out of town, over Cemetery Hill, on the Baltimore pike. All the way the houses, trees and thrown-down fences showed where the shot and shell had sped on their mission of death and destruction. The road was filled with army wagons, ambulances and wounded soldiers on their way to the railroad. Nearly every house had the red hospital flag, and here and there were stacks of guns which had been gathered from the battlefield. Off at the left of the road, in the edge of the woods, could be seen the newly-made graves of those who had fallen — members of the lst division of the 12th army corps. Some three miles from the town we passed the 11th army corps hospital, and about half a mile beyond, near a farm-house and a large barn, found the 12th army corps hospital.[36] They had good hospital tents, sufficiently large for six patients, but in each were from twelve to thirteen, lying on straw — for, as yet, no beds, pillows or bed-clothes of any kind had reached them. Most of them, fortunately, had their blankets. Their

---

36. The hospital consisted of the residence, barn, and the tents spread across the fields of the George Bushman farm along modern Route 15. The present house dates back to the time of the Civil War. The hospital was in operation from July 2 to July 21 when the remaining patients were moved to Camp Letterman. Gregory A. Coco, *A Vast Sea of Misery* (Gettysburg: Thomas Publications, 1988), pp. 102-4.

food consisted of hard-tack, meat and soup, which the weakest of the patients could not relish. Soon, however, this was remedied. I was assigned to duty in the first division, in which the greater part of the wounded were from the 27th Indiana and the 2d Massachusetts. There were many terrible cases of suffering. In one tent were two men who had lost both arms — one a member of the 20th Connecticut; the other a Michigan soldier. In one tent of the second division were nineteen cases of amputation — either a leg or an arm, or both.

The evening I reached the hospital, one of the surgeons wished me to go with him and see the major of the 66th Ohio,[37] who was fatally wounded through the chest. On entering the tent where he was he seemed very glad to see a lady, and said: "I remember having seen you at Acquia Creek." He shook my hand so cordially, and remarked: "I wish my sister at Rochester, N.Y., could come and take care of me." Before morning he needed no further care.

---

37. Major Joshua G. Palmer.

# V.

Sergeant William Blunt, of the 2d Massachusetts, only seventeen years of age, was a great sufferer from a mortal wound. As I entered the tent he said, looking round at the others: "None of you know what suffering is but me." He then prayed so earnestly that he might die. One morning, hearing my voice in the tent, he called, "Lady, come here!" He looked up so pleasantly and said, "My father has come." The surgeon in charge gave his father a small tent, to which his son was carried, and where he was made as comfortable as possible, his father watching anxiously by his side. His first words to his father were: "Oh, father, I've experienced religion, and am not afraid to die." He regretted that he had not another life to give for his country. He told his father that he wished to be buried in the bright folds of the stars and stripes. One afternoon, as I sat by him for a few minutes, speaking to him of the better land and the brighter home, he said: "I want you to pray for me when you pray." I told him I would; but in less than half an hour I was told "The old man's son has bled to death." An artery had sloughed, and he was no more.

> "To those who heard
> His dying word,
>     He died a hero bold;
> Tho' 'tis sweet to live,
> To country I give
>     My life — to God my soul."

Misses Bell, Dysart and Duncan soon joined us, and from early in the morn until late in the evening we went from tent to tent, doing with our might what our hands found to do for the comfort of those to whom we came to minister. The chaplains, too, were most faithful in attending to both the temporal and spiritual wants of the wounded.

When I first reached the 12th army corps hospital there were about eight hundred there, but in ten days' time the number was reduced to three hundred, some having died and others having left. Of those remaining quite a number were Confederates, and the orders were to take as good care of them as of our own wounded. "What, will you take care of me, too, lady?" was the inquiry of a wounded Confederate. "Yes," said I; "we treat you just as we want our boys treated when they are taken prisoners."

In one of the tents was John S. Lynch, of the 3d Alabama, in whom I became much interested. He was an earnest, simple christian, and his faith in God was so childlike. Then, too, he used to speak so tenderly of his mother. One day he said: "If my mother only knew how kind you are to me. It will kill my mother for me to die without her knowing of my fate. I believe the Almighty will restore me." But he was severely wounded in his right thigh and kept growing worse. The last rational words I heard him speak were: "Mother, you and I will meet in Heaven." In his porte-manteau [?] was found a piece of paper, on which were these lines:

> Work nor play on the Sabbath day,
> Neither idle away God's holy day;
> But think and sing of the Glorious King —
> Consider His goodness to every thing.
> Climb above to the land of love
> And seek the rest perpared[sic] for the blest,
> Where sleep the lambs on His breast.
>
> Walking in the somber light
> We know not we can live aright,
> He calls us to a land that's bright —
> His will be done; we know it's right.

I sent a letter by a flag of truce, giving her the particulars of his death, and after the war I learned that she received it.

About the 21st of July from one hundred and fifty to two hundred of the patients were moved to the general hospital, which was situated about three-fourths of a mile the other side of the town.[38] Miss Bell and I were ordered to go there and receive them as they were brought in. The most of them were carried on stretchers. There were six rows of tents and seventeen double hospital tents in a row. All the patients had good iron bedsteads, good mattresses, pillows, sheets, and everything needed for comfort. The surgeons and nurses all had tents, besides those of the Christian and Sanitary Commissions. The cooking-house — what part of it was not under a truss — was under a shed, and Miss Hall was in charge of it. Mrs. [Phebe M. (Agett)] May was assigned to the first ward, the writer to the second, Miss Dysart to the third, and Miss Bell to the fourth.

---

38. Camp Letterman.

A few days before we left the old camp a young Massachusetts boy had his leg amputated below the knee. He was under my special care, and with others was brought on a stretcher to this hospital, and I had him placed in Dr. [Henry C.] May's[39] ward, knowing he would receive the best of care. In a few days he became conscious that his recovery was doubtful, and wrote a farewell letter to his sister. The date was on the 24th, and on the 31st he — Corporal Theodore Butters, of the 2d Massachusetts — died. He was as brave and noble a youth as ever faced death on the battlefield. The Sunday following, his only sister, to whom he had written this letter, arrived, but too late to see her brother. Her heart was nearly broken on learning that he was dead and buried. In my own ward were four double tents, and I have kept a record of the names of all the inmates; how they were wounded, and the result in each case, so far as I could learn. August 3d we sat down to a table to eat for the first time in two weeks.

S. [Samuel] W. Woodman, of the 2d Massachusetts, from South Danvers, was in my ward, badly wounded in his left arm. Three times the surgeons thought of amputating it, but concluded he was too weak to endure it. We washed the wound with a strong acid, and gave him the best of care and diet. After awhile he commenced to improve, and we saw he was well enough to go on to Philadelphia to the hospital there. In January, 1866, I wrote to his mother to learn how he was, and received a reply, written by himself, that he was at home and apparently well.

On the 23rd of September the good people of Gettysburg and the surrounding towns made a grand festival for those remaining in the hospital. They brought chicken pies, bread, biscuits, butter, cakes, milk, ice-cream, fruits, &c. After dinner, the boys, as an evidence of their appreciation, did their best at games, running races, &c. It was a great day for them, and one long to be remembered by all.

Miss Dysart and I left Gettysburg October 23. The day before, we visited the battlefield for the first time. The general hospital was located on that part of the field where the Confederate General [Richard S.] Ewell's forces were stationed. All the way from that part to Culp's Hill nothing could then be seen except the ground here and there plowed up by the shells. Scattered about were stray knapsacks, bayonet sheaths, and a few unmarked graves, till we came near the breastworks which had been thrown

---

39. Henry C. May married Phebe Agett in 1859.

up by the 12th army corps — General [Henry Warner] Slocum's. From behind these fortifications must have issued a terrible storm of bullets, judging from the number of trees that had been struck and killed and the trenches in which were the Confederate dead. There, too, many of our boys received their wounds, as they had told me, and many fell, as the graves indicated, from New York, Pennsylvania, Ohio, Massachusetts, New Jersey, and Michigan. Under a tree in a field, was an only grave — that of Winfield Scott,[40] a dear boy from St. Lawrence county, N.Y. It was said that he was the only one killed in his regiment in that engagement. The winter before he was in our hospital at Harper's Ferry, and was loved by all. The day before we left Acquia Creek he came over to the hospital to see us.

The breastworks on Culp's Hill showed the location of the lst army corps, on the right wing of our army, at the left of the 12th army corps, during the last day's fighting. On the ridge to the left, we passed the place where the 11th army corps was stationed in the center. Proceeding through the cemetery, which was near where the 11th army corps had been stationed, down the Taneytown road, we came to the place where General [George G.] Meade had his headquarters, and where the shells came so fast. The effects were still very apparent. As we passed up the rise of ground, we came to where the 2d army corps had fought so desperately. On seeing the exposed position we did not wonder that the list of killed and wounded exceeded that of any other corps. From there we passed to where the 3d and 5th army corps held the field when the battle raged so terribly the last day, and where first were caught the words which were carried from corps to corps, "They are retreating." One dying man near Culp's Hill heard the shouting and asked what it meant. On being told, he said: "I am satisfied to die."

On Little Round Top, where the 3d army corps was, nature had built a strong defense for our men from the enemy's balls by piling rocks upon rocks, in the fissures of which could still be seen the remains of some of the Confederates — bleached by the weather.

Coming back to town from Little Round Top, we saw traces of fighting all the way. We passed the Peach Orchard, where so many of the New Hampshire boys fell in battle. Near the town we left the Emmittsburg road and crossed over to the Chambersburg road, where in a field, alone, was a little grave, on the headboard of which

---

40. Winfield W. Scott, Company C, 145th New York.

was simply inscribed, "Drummer Boy." No one knew his name, and perhaps his loving mother never learned of his death. Passing along, we came to the house of John Burns, that old man of seventy years who, on the first day of battle, took his gun, joined the 7th Wisconsin, and fought with them till he was wounded three times — the last wound disabling him. He was left on the field, but the next day managed to get back to his house. Some sympathizing (?) neighbors informed the Confederates what he had done. Soon after he was visited by some of their officers, and upon their leaving a ball came whizzing through the window, entering the wall just over his head. They evidently intended to kill him.

In the 1st army corps was the 147th New York, which lost so heavily, the first day, in killed and wounded. Among those killed was the gallant Lieutenant [Guilford D.] Mace, of Oswego county, N.Y. In childhood we were at school together, and there, after twenty years, I stood where he had given his life for his country.

At one time there were 2,000 of the wounded in the general hospital. When we left nearly all were gone. Many had died, and in the burying-ground near by were 300 graves.

> "And yet why weep
> For those that sleep
>         In a loyal soldier's grave?
> 'Tis enough to know
> Their blood did flow
>         For the cause of the good and brave."

# VI.

About the first of December, 1863, Miss Dysart and I secured passes to go to Nashville, Tenn., where Misses Hall and Bell had been for several weeks. On reaching Nashville we concluded it would be best for some of us to be nearer the front, so Miss Hall and I decided to go to Murfreesboro'. On going to the depot to take the train we found there was no passenger car attached, so we took passage with the train-guard in the "stockade car." The sides of this car were of thick plank, in which holes had been cut, so that in case the train was attacked the guard could repel the enemy's assault. At that time guerrillas frequently molested the trains.

We found Murfreesboro' a dismal-looking place, and the dire effects of war were everywhere visible. Two buildings that had formally been seminaries, several stores and a hotel, were being used for hospitals. These we found well filled with the sick and the wounded, and we concluded that there was enough for us to do.

We first called at the Sanitary Commission rooms, but found things scarcely settled there yet; so we applied to the Christian Commission, where we found two delegates and Chaplain [William] Earnshaw. The chaplain went with us to medical director, Dr. Israel Moses, who received us very coldly. He said all he should wish us to do, if we remained, would be to attend to the preparation of the low diet, and not enter the wards at all, and informed us that we could not be together in the same hospital.

At first we could not decide what to do. We were inclined to take the first train and return to Nashville, as our sphere for usefulness was to be so limited by the doctor; and even the chaplain thought we had better not stay, as we would meet with rebuffs and prejudice, and it would be rather lowering to our dignity to attend to the preparation of the diet. Knowing, however, that it was not generally considered beneath the dignity of a mother or a wife to prepare food for a sick son or a wounded husband, we concluded to remain and meet with determination whatever obstacles might be thrown in the way of our usefulness. There were many soldiers suffering for the want of proper care and food, as we had been told by one of the assistant surgeons, and if we could not care for them in the wards, we certainly could cook the food, in case we could secure the materials and rooms in which to do the cooking.

It was with difficulty that we found a place to stay the first night, for no one assisted us to secure lodgings; but at last we found a place with a Confederate woman by the name of Davis, a relative of the Confederate Colonel Ashley, of Virginia.[41]

## REPORTING FOR DUTY

The next morning we reported for duty. Miss Hall was assigned to No. 1, and the writer to No. 3 hospital. The surgeon at No. 1 went out and secured a room for us, and sent over two cot beds, some old blankets, sheets, pillows and mattresses — all very much soiled — as also a pail and wash basin, and we borrowed some bedding of the woman in whose house we had secured a room to supply our needs until we could get supplies from the Sanitary Commission.

On reporting to hospital No. 3, I was very coldly received by the surgeon in charge, but I found among the wounded quite a number of the 12th army corps boys, some of whom I had known in other hospitals. One said: "when I was down at Bridgeport I heard that you were out here somewhere, and I just said to one of the boys here that I thought Miss Dada would come soon." Another New York soldier said: "I am glad to see a New York lady." Another asked if I intended to remain. I replied "Yes." "Thank God," said he.

Most of the patients had been wounded at Lookout Mountain, but some were still suffering from wounds received in that bloody battle of Chickamauga; so, upon the whole, we were not sorry that we had remained, notwithstanding that we received no encouragement from anyone who wore shoulder straps.[42] The sick and wounded regretted as well as we that we were restricted to preparing food and distributing it through the different wards.

Soon after I went to the Christian Commission to see if I could get some eggs for one of the patients, who was very low, and needed something besides hard-tack and coffee, but I found that they had none, and did not show any disposition to try to get any. All that the patients at that time had for supper was bread, apple sauce, and tea. I told Dr. Douglas,[43] the ward surgeon and a Chris-

---

41. Possibly the famous Turner Ashby of Fauquier County Virginia who became a Brigadier General in May of 1862.
42. The Battle of Lookout Mountain was fought November 24, 1863; Chickamauga, September 19 and 20, 1863.
43. Probably Doctor Addison C. Douglass.

tian gentlemen, that I would gladly prepare some food if materials and a place to cook could only be furnished. He said: "I will see that you have some chickens to-morrow, if they will allow you to prepare them in the full-diet kitchen." I called upon the head cook and found him to be Nicholas Anderson, who formerly had been cook at the 12th army corps hospital in Gettysburg. He very willingly consented, and offered to assist me all he could.

About the 22d of December some supplies were brought on, and a stove was given me, with a colored woman and a little girl to assist. We prepared food for about forty. The boys thought that everything tasted so much better. For fifty cents per gallon I also succeeded in obtaining some milk, which made a substantial diet for those who were very low.

## WELCOME AID

Mrs. Lee, from Elk Horn, Wis., visited our hospital about this time and became very much interested in all that concerned the comfort of our soldiers, and in February following, I received from the Woman's Aid Society, of Elk Horn, a draft for $25 and during the year a number of them, and afterwards one for $50, to be used as I saw fit, for the relief of those under my care. From other sources I also received at different times sums of money with which to buy delicacies for the sick.

In January Dr. May, now of Corning, N.Y., one of the surgeons at Gettysburg of whom I have spoken, arrived from Nashville. While in town he called upon the medical director, and, in the course of his conversation, said he was acquainted with two of the ladies in the hospitals there. The medical director answered contemptuously: "Ladies! There are no ladies in the hospitals here. The hospital is no place for a lady. We have some women here who are cooks."

The 1st of February Miss Tuttle came on, and was assigned to No. 2 hospital. We were kept very busy in preparing food and distributing it among so many. Often we wrote letters for the patients to inform their friends where they were, and the condition of their wounds, &c. One day an old Tennessee woman came in from the country, and on inquiring why she was so sad, she told me that her son, who had been a noted scout, and who had often piloted our army in Tennessee, had been brutally murdered by the bushwhackers, a little more than a week before. They had threatened to burn the mother's house if she went after her son's body, but she had bravely replied: "You may kill me if you will, and burn my house; I am for the Union, and shall die for it," and, despite their threats she had taken the body home and, after keeping it two days, had buried it. The tears ran down her furrowed cheeks as she told me how nice his hair was combed, and how sweet he looked — her own dear boy.

During the latter part of the winter and early spring interesting religious meetings were held at the Christian Commission rooms every evening, which were productive of much good. Not a few of those in the hospitals were led to believe on the Lord Jesus Christ, which not only brought joy to Christians there, but also to their friends at home.

# VII.

As spring came on, all who were able for duty were ordered to the front. Those in No. 3 hospital, with which I was connected, who were not able to go to the front were sent to No. 1 hospital. On the 18th of May my hospital was closed, and on the afternoon of the 22d of May I took the train for Chattanooga, leaving Miss Hall to follow when I should send for her.

## CHATTANOOGA

Hospital No. 1 at Chattanooga was composed of eight one-story and four two-story wooden buildings, besides a large number of tents. The wooden structures were built by the Confederate General [Braxton] Bragg, and situated on a hill near to and including a brick building that had formerly been an academy. I found Dr. F. [Francis] Salter in charge of the hospital. He had been in charge at Winchester, Va., when I was there, two years before. He received me most cordially, and immediately wrote to Miss Hall, asking her to come at once.

Car-loads of the wounded were daily being brought in from the front, but all who were able to bear transportation were sent on farther north, and only the most severely wounded were left there — such as were brought on stretchers.

I was assigned to the second division of the hospital, which was composed of eight one-story buildings, with twenty-four beds each, and three two-story buildings, with forty-eight beds each, making 336 beds. I went through every building and spoke with each patient, which took me a whole day. I desired to survey the field and to see what there was to be done.

While passing through one of the wards, I found a young man who had been wounded through the leg and was very low indeed, and noticed that the usual card giving his name and the address of his parents had not been placed at the head of his bed. I asked him for the necessary information. He said: "I wish they had taken that leg off, but I suppose some must go with the cause." That afternoon he died. His name was [Sylvester] Aborn, and he belonged to the 2d Massachusetts.

Never was I in a hospital where there was so much suffering as at Chattanooga, and never was I more kindly received by the surgeons, nor were my services ever more appreciated by the sick and wounded. Often, as I passed through the wards, the tears would dim the eyes of the patients, as they spoke of a wife, or a mother, or a sister at home, and showed me the photograph of some dear one that they had sacredly preserved.

It would be impossible for me to write of all the heartrending scenes that were witnessed during this month of June and the months which followed. It seemed as if the "Angel of Death" was constantly hovering over the hospital. On the first day there were thirteen deaths.

One of the two-story buildings was used as the gangrene ward. The dressing of the wounds of those who had gangrene caused the most intense suffering, and there were several deaths daily. As fast as the beds were vacated by death other cases were brought in — some directly from the front and others from the different hospitals.

## AN UNHYGIENIC SURGEON

Although the buildings were well arranged for ventilation, yet there was one old surgeon who ordered all the ventilators in his ward closed every night. The result was that we had more cases of gangrene from that ward than any other. The weather was very warm, and every precaution should have been taken for the comfort and safety of the wounded, yet this old surgeon seemed to ignore every sanitary law. It was found that the occurrence of so many deaths in a single ward had an unfavorable effect on the health of those who survived, and for that reason a tent was placed in front of the building, a short distance away, and to it, from time to time, all cases apparently past recovery were taken. But one soldier of all who were taken there recovered. In the gangrene ward was a lad from Michigan named Martin Howell.[44] He had lost both legs below the knee. "Oh," said he, "I have been a wild boy, and I do not know that I should ever have been led to think of my soul had I not been stopped in this way," and as he spoke the tears filled his blue eyes. By his side was Nation Gooley, who had lost a leg. Yet both seemed in good spirits, rejoiced over General [William T.] Sherman's successful advance, and said: "We willingly give what we have lost for the old flag." In a few weeks Martin Howell was sleeping in the National Cemetery at Chattanooga: the other died while friends were taking him home.[45]

---

44. Isaac M. Howell, Company C, 23rd Michigan Infantry.
45. Nation Gooley, Company C, 73rd Ohio Infantry died on a boat at Cincinnati, Ohio.

As I entered the ward the morning of the 3d of June I found that Andrew Lillie[46] had just died. He had been brought in only two days before. His leg had been amputated, but while being brought in from the front, the gangrene had made such progress that his life could not be saved. The day before his death I wrote a letter home for him. Often it was found necessary to amputate a leg or an arm the second time, and in such cases it seemed a wonder that any one recovered. There were so many that were very low, that I was obliged to buy milk for them, for which I had to pay fifty cents per quart. I felt that these dying men ought to have every thing that could be obtained which would add to their comfort and show our appreciation of what they had done and suffered for their country.

At the moment of writing this I am in receipt of a letter from Thomas Gilmore of Harrison, Ill., who belonged to the 107th N.Y.V. He lost a leg at Dallas, Ga., May 25, 1864. He was in this gangrene ward at the time of which I am writing. He says in this letter:

> Do you remember me and Charles Frank,[47] Samuel Harrison,[48] Moses Garabrant, and the other inmates of the gangrene ward, who, like myself, had each lost a leg? Garabrant died on the bed next to me. What terrible times those were; and how many of our comrades were carried out of that ward to the cemetery every night. I came pretty near going myself. How glad we were to see your face coming into the ward every morning, and how nobly you did your duty — writing letters home for the boys, furnishing stationery and stamps, carrying delicacies to the very sick, forwarding letters after we had been transferred, &c., &c.

Sergeant Livingston[49] was among those brought into the gangrene ward. He had been seriously wounded by a shell in the left thigh and it soon became evident that he, too, must yield up his young life, so full of hope and promise. A lieutenant's commission had been promised him. I found that he was not disposed to be very communicative, and it was with difficulty that I succeed in getting him to dictate a few lines to the loved ones at home. I remember that it was a hot summer day, and I sat by the bedside with my pencil and paper. The surgeon had said that there might be one chance for him, and that he must take all the beef tea he

---

46. Andrew Lillie, Company H, 85th Indiana Infantry.
47. Charles Frank, Company H, 149th New York Infantry.
48. Samuel Harrison, Company A, 149th New York Infantry.
49. Sergeant George W. Livingston, Company I, 19th Michigan Infantry.

could, so, with a nervous grasp, he seized the bottle in which was the tea and, drinking a few swallows, dictated the following letter:

> Dear parents: I am still here, though very low. There may yet be some chance for me to recover. I shall yet hope. There is One who alone can restore me, and He alone can prepare me for the future world. The doctor has just told me that there was a possible chance. I shall try for it. You may always be satisfied that I have not showed one bit of cowardice on the field of battle. It can never be said of your son that he fell back before he heard the word "Retreat," unless it was to assist some wounded man. He has shown no cowardice whatever.

This was all he dictated. He failed rapidly, and soon his bed was vacant and his remains were sleeping in one of the soldiers' cemeteries. I sent the letter to his parents, who were living in St. Joseph, Mich., and added whatever I thought would be of interest.

Miss Hall came on to assist on the 12th of June. She was assigned to four of the one-story buildings. About that time the 5th and 7th Ohio regiments passed through Chattanooga, on their way home, having been in the service three years and three months. Some of the boys I had known at Winchester more than two years before; others, at Harper's Ferry, Washington, Acquia Creek and Gettysburg. They had heard that Miss Hall and I were there, and so they gave us a call. They had passed through many a battle and made many a long march, and they had left behind them, quietly sleeping beneath the sod in Virginia, Tennessee and Georgia, many a brave comrade. We saw that they were carrying home honorable badges — the scars of wounds received in battle, — and we could not but feel for them that reverence, mingled with gratitude, which they deserved from every loyal heart. Among those who fell asleep in Jesus during this month were Duncan Thompson, of the 64th Ohio; William Coleman of the 63rd Indiana, and Andrew[sic] Everitt,[50] of the 124th Ohio. The last named was severely wounded through his body. He gave directions as to what should be done with his effects, and talked tenderly of the loved ones at home. Implicitly trusting in the Lord Jesus Christ, he calmly fell asleep. At times, all night long, from different parts of the camp could be heard the groans of the restless wounded. How often were we called upon to write to friends at home, "Your son died;" "Your husband is dead;" "Your brother has fallen asleep."

---

50. I believe this should be Ambrose Everitt.

And in some instances, I presume, not so much as this brief word ever reached their friends. Some of the boys in their last delirium would cry out: "Mother! Mother!" Such suffering cannot be conceived except by those who either bore or witnessed it.

Daily I saw devoted Christian young men dying on their country's altar — costly sacrifice — men that the country could not well afford to spare. Many a heart and home were made desolate, while heaven seemed to be garnering rich treasures.

"You will receive your reward;" "God bless you," and similar expressions daily fell from the lips of the sufferers to whom I have ministered — expressions of their appreciation and thankfulness. Surely, I did receive my reward. Three years had passed, during which time I had enjoyed almost uninterrupted health, and it had been my privilege to minister to the sick and wounded soldiers — one of the greatest privileges given to an American woman. I shall always prize the many letters I received from the friends of those to whom I ministered, so full of gratitude — the out-gushings of loving hearts — thanking me for the services rendered to a dear husband, son, or brother. These letters I have kept all these years; and even now, on looking them over, they vividly bring to my mind many a sad scene, and the looks, as well as the words, of some of those who now enjoy a calm and undisturbed repose.

There were twenty deaths on the last day of June, and during the month 261, in a hospital where there were only about seven hundred beds. But it should be remembered that almost daily patients were sent to Nashville and others were brought in. Some of those who were brought in died in a few hours; others, in a few days.

> "Some things are worthless,
> Some others so good.
> That nations who buy them
> Pay only in blood."

# VIII.

During the summer of 1864, while at Chattanooga, Tenn., a soldier by the name of Redd,[51] from Vinton county, Ohio, severely wounded below the knee, was brought to our hospital from the front. From the first I feared that he, too, would soon be numbered with those who had sealed their patriotism with their blood; but the surgeons thought otherwise, and the wounded man himself was hopeful. Day after day passed, but there was no improvement. One morning, as I entered the ward, I saw that his hours were numbered, and that soon "the silver cord would be loosed." I had often talked with him about his wife and children, and had learned, too, that he was a Christian, but I could not, I thought, tell him how near he was to the Christian's home. So, meeting the chaplain of the hospital — a good man, I told him my patient could not live long, and asked him to inform him of his situation. The chaplain soon returned and said: "I have done as you wished, and the man is ready to go, trusting in Christ." I went to his bedside. His mind was so weak that he did not seem to realize he was near his end. He simply said he was comfortable and felt no pain. That forenoon he received a letter from his family. I immediately offered to write an answer for him, wishing to take down his last words for those who were so dear to him. It was with great effort that he summoned strength for the task. He said:

> Dear Wife and Daughter: I have just received your kind and welcome letter, dated the 11th. I have an opportunity to get a Christian lady to write to you, and I embrace it at once. I would say again, I have good nurses, good attention and doctors, who I think understand my case; yet I will not attempt to express the idea that I am entirely out of danger. A soldier, when wounded, is not free from danger. The only real safety is in the religion of the Bible, which has thus far sustained me.

"Let me sleep a little now," said he. After a while he resumed:

> Jennie, I want you to be good, kind and obedient to your mother. Oh, remember this! I ask you not to owe special obedience to this minister or that minister, but to your mother and to your God, who has said, " I will never leave thee nor forsake thee." Dear wife, my

---

51. Franklin Redd, Company C, 73rd Ohio Infantry. Wife was named Elizabeth.

motive was good in coming out. I trust God will not hold me accountable for any improper motive. Oh, put your trust in God! He will never leave nor forsake you. Thank God for that precious promise. He is verifying it to me now. "I will never leave thee nor forsake thee." I trust he will verify it to you also.

He would frequently fall asleep, and it was with difficulty that I aroused him to send some word to his little boy. He directed me to write:

Dear Dockey, be a good, kind, obedient, religious boy.

Again he closed his eyes, and I left him for a few moments, but on returning I found his spirit had returned to God who gave it.

Charles Emerson, of the 97th Ohio, died on the 18th July. The first day he was brought to the hospital he said he was so glad to see me — to think I had come to take care of poor soldiers. On the same day died Robert Redmond, of the 23rd Michigan. He had been there a long time, and was a patient sufferer. On the 19th, 21st, 24th and 28th of July, there were five deaths each day in my wards. Some days there were three deaths in the gangrene ward, and on one day there were six.

On the 19th of July, Sergeant Wm. H. Yates[52] died — as brave a soldier as Kentucky ever furnished to the cause. He was wounded by a shell, which broke his thigh. All was done that could be to save his life. Wm. C. Harris, of the 94th Ohio, died on the same day. He was in the hospital when I first went there. He had been wounded in the left arm, and several inches of the bone had been removed. Cheerfully he bore it all, and pictured to himself a bright and happy future. We thought he would soon be able to bear the journey home, but he began to fail, gangrene set in and all efforts to save him were unavailing. He had no fears of death, for he believed in the Lord Jesus Christ. He only wished to live for his mother, as one brother had been murdered by the guerrillas while on his way home from the army. Those who took care of W. C. Harris will long remember him.

## CHEERING THE DESPONDENT

Among those who were brought in was a man from an Ohio regiment, who was dangerously wounded in his arm. When he was about to be transferred to Nashville he had a severe hemor-

---

52. William H. Yates, Company H, 20th Kentucky Infantry.

rhage, and it was decided to amputate the arm. A few days later gangrene made its appearance. One evening, as the wound was being dressed, he looked up to me and said: "There is no use in trying, I can't endure it." Wishing to arouse him and to excite greater courage, I said: "You, a man with a family, and talking that way!" Saying no more, I left him. In the morning he greeted me with hearty thanks for the reproof. Never again was he known to give up, and in a few weeks he was on his way home. If a patient gave up all hope he was almost sure to die; therefore, it was necessary to inspire courage.

On the 21st of July occurred the death of William Dougherty, of the 109th Pennsylvania, who had lost both legs above the knee. He was a great sufferer, but died trusting in Christ. On the same night George F. Boughman, of the 147th Pennsylvania died. He had but a slight wound in his right foot, but through the ignorance of that unhygienic surgeon to whom I referred in my last article, gangrene made such headway that amputation was necessary, and death soon followed. The next to go were Hiram Rogers,[53] suffering from a wound in the thigh, who wasted away to a mere skeleton; Thorn Case, of the 21st Ohio, and Benjamin F. Bennett, of the 10th Illinois. The latter was in the hospital when I first went there. He had been wounded in the thigh. He seemed to be doing well till this remarkable old surgeon removed the splints, after which he failed rapidly. Robert Huchinson [sic],[54] of the 21st Ohio, was the next to go. Another of our patients was Charles S. Scott, fife major of the 37th [sic][55] Indiana. He had gone up to the rifle-pits to see how the boys were getting along, and had been there hit with a ball. He was brought to our hospital with his leg amputated. For some time we thought he would recover, but he was taken with chills, and soon after died.

## MORE WOUNDED

On the 28th of this month — July, 1864 — quite a number of wounded men were brought to our hospital from the scenes of the late battles. Among them were several from the 22nd Wisconsin, which regiment had been stationed at Murfreesboro' the winter before, and some of them I knew. Sumner Nelson of that regi-

---

53. Hiram Rogers, Company E, 19th Michigan Infantry.
54. Hutchinson.
55. 36th Indiana.

ment, was brought in with a leg amputated. I also found Corporal William Bright,[56] now of Utica, N.Y., whom we thought was dead, as we had heard he had been wounded and left on the field. His right arm was gone and he was severely wounded through his side. I had him taken to my ward. The doctors thought there was but little chance for his recovery, but in a few weeks he was able to leave the hospital and go home.

There were not so many deaths in July and August: still, some died every day. In August two wards were used for gangrene patients. Captain [John Q.] Mercer, of the 147th Pennsylvania, was very low, and the surgeons thought he could not recover; but in September we saw him able to leave the hospital, and a few months after he wrote us: "I think that if it had not been for your care, last summer, I would now be lying beneath a little mound near Chattanooga." His was certainly one of the most remarkable cases of recovery I ever knew.

Ormandus[sic] Silsby[57] died August 30th. He was an interesting boy, born in Siam, where his father was a missionary. His father was also in the army — a lieutenant in a Wisconsin battery, stationed at Chattanooga, so that he was often able to see his son.

Albert J. Martin, of Ohio,[58] died on the 5th of September. His message home was: "Tell them I died in the faith of Christ; that I never have publicly professed it, but I intended to do so." Peacefully he passed away and "was not, for God took him."

When the news reached the hospital that General Sherman had taken Atlanta, there was great rejoicing through the wards. Some who had lost one or both legs wished they could have entered the city with their comrades.

I received word to go to the 20th army corps hospital at Atlanta, but was unable to secure a pass.

Lieutenant James McQuillan[59] died October 2. He was wounded through the thigh near the artery. He nearly bled to death when they tied the artery. The circulation not being good, his foot began to mortify, and he could not be saved. He was told he could not recover, and, having calmly made his preparations for death, fell asleep, trusting in the Lord Jesus Christ.

---

56. Corporal William H. Bright, Company C, 22nd Wisconsin Infantry.
57. Sergeant Amandus Silsby, Company A, 24th Wisconsin Infantry. Father John belonged to lst Wisconsin Heavy Artillery, Battery C.
58. Albert J. Martin, Co. F, 82nd Ohio Infantry.
59. Lieutenant James McQuillen, Company I, 38th Ohio Infantry.

Among those who left the hospital about the 20th of October, was George Moreland, of Indiana.[60] He had been there since the 26th of February, — eight months, — badly wounded in the thigh and side. I received a letter from him recently, stating he had never fully recovered. In this same ward in which he lay so long, death had claimed a victim from every bed except his, and from some of them several. There were only fifty-nine deaths in the hospital in October.

On the last of October and the 1st of November they began to bring in the wounded from Atlanta. Among them was Henry Potter,[61] now of Washington, D.C., who was wounded through the right knee at Jonesboro'[Jonesborough], about the first of September.[62] His leg was not amputated until May, 1865. The beds were soon all filled again and some were laid on the floor. A number were brought in dead, having expired on the cars. Others died soon after reaching the hospital. The weather was damp and chilly. As yet there were no stoves in the hospital, and it was difficult to prevent those who were very low from suffering from the cold. Hot drinks had to be made for them. To one I gave some warm tea at dinner time. I told him I was fearful he would be no better. He thought otherwise, not realizing how very low he was. About two hours afterwards I went to the same ward again. He had died in the interval and had been carried out, and another patient was in his place.

There were one hundred and fifty-three deaths in the month of November in this hospital. People in their comfortable homes can form no idea of the suffering there was in that hospital at this time. The patients, weary, exhausted, suffering from sickness and wounds, all night long would lie there in those dreary wards, thinking of loved ones far away at home, while they, the victims of that cruel war, were suffering and many of them dying there. No one but God knows the anguish — the death pangs — they suffered who sealed their patriotism with their blood.

---

60. George Moreland, Company I, 82nd Indiana Infantry.
61. Sergeant Henry G. Potter, Company A, 74th Indiana Infantry.
62. The Battle of Jonesborough, Georgia, August 31– September 1, 1864.

## IX.

From the latter part of November till the 25th of December 1864, the Confederates were between us at Chattanooga and Nashville. All this time we were without any mail, and were quite in the dark concerning the movements of the enemy. At the hospital all had plenty to eat; but at the camps around they were on half rations.

Many refugees from Georgia were encamped at the time near Chattanooga, on their way North; but, as all communication had been cut off, they could proceed no farther. There was much suffering among them and many died from exposure.

One day as I was passing through one of the wards, a man wearing a white star on his cap spoke to me. I recognized him as Chauncey Pease, one of the 60th New York, whom I had known at Acquia Creek. He was a most faithful nurse, and, I might add, there were many excellent nurses among those who were assigned to that work. I am not able to recall the names of many, but some of them will not be forgotten by those for whom they cared.

About the 10th of January Misses Bell and [Sallie E.] Chamberlain, who had been visiting us, from the hospitals in Nashville, left, taking with them Miss Dysart, who had been with us about two months. Miss Dysart had had charge of the diet kitchen. She was succeeded by Miss Tuttle. I then had two sections to visit, consisting of 192 beds. In one section all were sick with measles. Many were new recruits, and they got sick very easily, — especially the conscripts, — and seemed discouraged and low spirited. One boy said: "If I should get well, I would have to go to my regiment, and I would as soon die." He never had been with his regiment; or, if so, only for a short time. It often happened that those apparently nearly recovered from the disease would grow careless, suffer a relapse, and die.

One poor fellow, whose name I do not remember, was brought into my ward very sick with pneumonia. The regimental surgeon had said nothing was the matter with him; so he did not get the care he needed till he came to the hospital, and then it was too late. Many a life was similarly sacrificed.

Peter Horan,[63] a mere boy, with sandy hair and freckled face, died in my ward. He belonged to one of the Northern States —

---

63. Peter Horan, Company G, 149th Illinois Infantry.

which one I cannot call to mind. Knowing that he had no relations or friends to whom I could write, I cut off a lock of his hair, which I still have, that he might not be wholly forgotten.

One poor boy, whose measles had settled on his lungs, and who lived less than two days after he was brought to the hospital, would call out: "Woman!" every time I entered the ward, and once added this very strange expression: "You are the God blessedest woman I ever saw." The only morning he was there I gave him his breakfast — the little tea that he was able to take — and he asked: "You will stay with me all day, wont you?" I was sorry to tell him there were other sick ones who would be looking for me, and I must go and see them. He soon became delirious, and in a few hours was dead. He had been away from home but a few weeks. Another, who had been very sick with inflammation of the lungs, and for whom I had prepared some stewed dried peaches, said: "You are the best woman I ever saw."

A soldier spoke to me as I was passing through the ward whom I did not recognize. "Where have I known you before?" I inquired. "At Winchester," he replied. He was wounded and taken prisoner at the time of Banks' retreat, and I well remember when he was brought in from the battlefield. He improved rapidly, went home, and received his discharge, but in a year or so afterwards he volunteered again in the same regiment.

### VISITING THE WARDS

The morning of March 19th was beautiful, and I thought I would write home, as I seldom had an opportunity. After I had swept and dusted my room, I concluded to visit the wards first. I took some papers to distribute, a can of tomatoes, which I had got from the Christian Commission, and a bottle of blackberry wine from the Indiana State agency. I entered my own ward — No. 1 — a two-story building, consisting of twenty-four beds in each story, and the first man I came to was a German, belonging to the 188th Ohio, who had been sick a long time with chronic diarrhea and was very weak. Next to him was Wilson, who had been there about three months, suffering with liver complaint. He looked badly, and we knew he could never recover unless by a change of climate; so he was put down for a discharge. Next to him was a man who was very sick when first brought there, but was then able to walk about a little. Next to him was a boy sick and delirious. A day or two before he asked me: "Which would you rather have — a coon or a 'possum?" He then asked for one my papers to read. I gave him a child's paper, and a Fulton paper to a New York boy a little farther on. Just across the ward was a Kentucky soldier, who had been in the service ever since the commencement of the war. He was completely worn out, had a low fever, and was unconscious most of the time. Beside him was a man who had been improving and feeling quite well until the night before, when he had been taken with a cough, followed suddenly by a hemorrhage of the lungs. I went on up stairs, and one of the patients asked me to send him for his dinner some soup made of water, butter, pepper and salt, with crackers broken in it. I happened to have some crackers, for which I had paid thirty cents a pound, so he got the dinner he ordered.

In ward 2 they were all convalescent and most of them able to sit up. In ward 3 a few wounded were still left. During the summer before that had been the gangrene ward where so many died. In each of these two-story buildings, which had been assigned to me, there were forty-eight beds, yet scarcely one on which I could not recall that some one had died, while on some several deaths had occurred.

One section I was not able to visit that day till after supper. One dear young boy, sick with measles, said: "I was afraid you had left. I dreamed last night that you came and gave me two lemons." "Oh," said I, "you want some lemonade, do you?" I told him I could not get any lemons, but I would prepare a drink for him, and the last thing I did was to prepare and carry it to him.

## HIGH PRICES

It was with difficulty that we procured delicacies for those who were very sick. We could scarcely get chickens at any price-never for less than one dollar each. Eggs were from sixty to eighty cents per dozen; milk was fifty cents per quart, and one day I paid one dollar for a pail of potatoes. At times they were five dollars per bushel. I felt very grateful to the friends at the North and West who sent me funds with which to buy these necessaries for the sick and wounded.

On the 22d of March 1865, a man named Ellis,[64] belonging to the 1st Wisconsin battery, died in my ward. His younger brother, a member of the same battery, came to the hospital in great dis-

---

64. Edward D. Ellis, D, 1st Wisconsin Heavy Artillery, company C. Brother was named Birch Ellis.

tress, as this was the third brother he had lost in the army. He said he wished to send the body home, but he had not been paid off in a long time and did not have enough money. His home was in Moravia, near Auburn, N.Y. It happened that I had some money with me, which I felt I could spare for a while, so I let him have it, and directed him to Mr. Reed, of the Sanitary Commission, knowing he would render him assistance in getting a coffin. I also asked one of the ward surgeons to embalm his brother's remains, which he did. The next evening the brother called, and told me how well he had succeeded in arranging everything.

On the afternoon of March 23, 1865, Miss Hall and I took dinner at Dr. [Lewis] Applegate's. He was soon to leave Chattanooga. We had chicken pie, the first I had eaten in at least two years, and we also had some poached eggs — the only time I had ever eaten any at Chattanooga, unless it was at Dr. Salter's, when I first went there, ten months before. I merely mention this that the reader may know that our diet during those years in the hospitals was of the plainest and simplest character and included no delicacies. Many a time all that I had to eat was toasted bread with salt sprinkled on it, wet with water, and a cup of coffee; and sometimes only a dish of gruel. There were times, too, when I hardly had time to eat even that.

During the month of March there were eighty-two deaths in the hospital, — fifty-three of them in my ward, — and thirty-seven of the fifty-three were from measles.

### CHEERING NEWS

April the 3d news came to the hospital that Richmond had been taken by our troops at 8:15 a.m. This news cheered every heart and seemed to impart vigor to many of the soldiers. Troops at that time were daily passing through Chattanooga on the cars. Among them were those of General [George Henry] Thomas, on their way to North Carolina. As the cars stopped, some of our old soldier friends would often give us a call. They were from Minnesota, Wisconsin, Illinois, Indiana, and Ohio, and all seemed like old friends.

April 10 news came that General [Robert E.] Lee and his army had surrendered. Guns were fired and engines whistled in honor of the event, and on the 14th Secretary [Edwin M.] Stanton ordered all recruiting to be stopped. Still, in the hospital almost every day some died. At noon, on the 15th of April, all our joy was turned into the deepest grief by the sad intelligence that Abraham Lincoln, our beloved and honored President, had been assassinated the evening before, and had died that morning. It cast a gloom over all to know that he had been stricken down by the hand of an assassin. The news spread rapidly. A little colored boy came to our door, knocked, and with eyes as well as voice expressed it all. Said he: "Mr. President Lincum is dead." The lad could not retain his feelings, and wanted us to share with him the sad news.

April 20 Charles K. Baldwin, from Pilot Grove, Iowa,[65] a very patient sufferer, died from the effect of a wound through his right shoulder. He had been brought to the hospital on the 2d of the preceding November. I informed his aged mother of his death. His sister wrote me, and from her letter I quote:

"Charles was an only son and brother, and as such was almost idolized. Well did he deserve our love, for he was a most obedient and affectionate son, and a kind, loving and indulgent brother. He was, for many years after father's death, our all; and, being the eldest by several years, he was, in one sense, both father and brother to my sister and myself. It is very hard indeed that our only brother should be taken from us. It seems as if our hearts would break, and still we would not call him back if we could. Upon mother the blow has fallen heavily, as she is getting to be old. Sad, sad tidings: They will cause us to mourn the remainder of our days, be they few or many."

---

65. Charles K. Baldwin, Company I, 17th Iowa Infantry.

# X.

On May 9, 1865, Miss Hall and I received our beautiful corps badge. It consisted of a gold cross surmounted with a crown, studded with pearls, and pendent from the cross was a star of gold, on one side of which was inscribed: "Inasmuch as ye have done it unto one of the least of these, my brethren, ye have done it unto me." On the other side: "Presented to Hattie A. Dada by the medical officers of the 12th army corps."[66]

On the 10th we visited the famous battlefield of Lookout Mountain, where General [Joseph] Hooker and his brave army fought above the clouds. We saw Picket Rock and the large spring underneath, where our troops obtained water the night after the battle, and also the rocky ledge, from which triumphantly floated the stars and stripes the next morning. As fast as the boys were able they left the hospital for their regiments, as the war was over, and many were being mustered out of the service.

About this time there were some quite sudden deaths in section 6 of the hospital, the result of medicine given by a young doctor. Some, who refused to take his medicine, got well!

Miss Hall and I commenced packing our trunks, so as to be ready to go home at the first opportunity. On the morning of the 24th of May we concluded we would take the train that afternoon. I visited all my wards, and found a few very sick. Miss Hall was not able to visit her wards. The four years of constant work and anxiety in caring for the sick and wounded had told on her health, and she has never fully recovered from it. It was a mental strain and nervous tax which but few could endure. I gave out dinner that day as usual. Bidding them good-by, we took the train for Nashville, but owing to delays did not get there till the next day in the afternoon. It was our expectation, on leaving Chattanooga, to spend a few days with friends in Shelbyville, Ill., and, after attending the great fair of the Sanitary Commission, which was to be held in Chicago in June, to go to our homes in New York State. But on our return from Chicago to Shelbyville we found letters, saying that all the ladies but one had left the hospital at Chatta-

---

66. Another source has the inscription as follows: "Inasmuch as ye have done unto one of the least of these ye have done it unto me." Dwight H. Bruce, *Onondaga's Centennial* (The Boston History Company. Publishers. 1896), Vol. II, Part III, Family Sketches, p. 16.

nooga, and there was no one to visit the wards, whereupon I sent word to telegraph me if they wished me to return, and receiving a telegram June 23d, I started that evening for the hospital. Miss Hall did not accompany me, but went on East, and placed herself under medical care. She had been absent from home four years.

## WELCOME BACK

On my return I was most cordially received, and I never regretted that I went back, for not a day passed but some one would say: "How good it is to have a lady here." During my absence a large number of the patients that I knew had left the hospital and some had died. Others, however, were still very sick, and so I was kept busy.

Charles Emerson of the 97th Ohio, died on the 18th of July. I well remember, the first day he was brought to the hospital, how glad he was to see me. On the same day died Robert Redmond, of the 23d Michigan. He had been there a long time and was a patient sufferer. The 19th, 21st, 24th, and 28th of July there were five deaths each day in my wards.

July 22d Mr. Messenger died.[67] His greatest anxiety had been to see his wife once more. I had written to her to come on while I still had hopes of his recovery. He was a Christian and died happily in the Lord. At my request the body was not sent to the cemetery that day, and at night his wife arrived. An acquaintance persuaded her to remain at the hotel while he went up to the hospital. There he learned the sad news, but kept it from her until the following morning. She was crushed by the news, and I went with her to the dead house, where her husband's remains were lying. He was greatly emaciated and she could hardly recognize him. That afternoon I took an ambulance and accompanied her to the burial. There was no chaplain in attendance — no one present, indeed, except the wardmaster, the mother of a sick boy, a Mrs. Mehan, and the steward from Lookout Mountain. The remains of two other patients were interred at the same time, and a company of colored troops fired three volleys over the graves. Poor, sorrowing woman! I wondered how she could endure it — so strange a funeral it must have seemed to her.

---

67. William B or G Messenger, Company F, 186 Ohio Infantry. His wife was named Harriet.

That evening quite a number of soldiers were mustered out of service, whose names I had taken, and in the morning I put up luncheons for them and they started for home.

The last of July and first of August quite a large number of new patients were brought in, but as soon as they were able to leave they were mustered out.

On the forenoon of August 6th George Hall, of Minnesota, I think, died.[68] About an hour before he aroused from his death-like slumber and sang with the chaplain, in a clear voice, "There'll be no more sorrow there." He then said: "I wish to sing a verse that mother used to have me sing and that uncle sang before he died." He asked the chaplain to sing it with him. It was the well-known hymn: "A light in the window for thee, brother." He next asked the chaplain — Mr. Stivers — to pray with him, and repeating after him a few words, soon sank into a sleep from which there was to be no awakening in this world. Early in the morning of the day he died he sent for me and said his father, who had been with him for several days, had told him that he was dying. He wanted to thank me for all my kindness and bid me good-by.

On the evening of August 10th eighty-six patients left on [the] hospital train, and thirty-eight new ones came. The hospital could not yet be closed. The weather was very warm, and the water poor and scarce. If there had been no more rain the year before, our sick and wounded soldiers would have suffered much more than they did.

Fielding Catt[69] died on the 4th of September. He had been sick most of the time after my return, and before his wife came on (five or six days before he died) he would say to me, "I want you to speak to me every time you come into the ward." He was buried the next day. I notified Chaplain [Thomas B.] Van Horn, and he was at the grave and made a few remarks and prayed.

For several weeks in August and September one building was filled with colored soldiers, whom I visited daily. One colored man said to me a day or two before he died, "I shall get home first," and he surely did.

---

68. There is a George H. Hall in F battery, 1st Minnesota Heavy Artillery who died in the Chattanooga hospital. He died however, on April 12, 1865.
69. Fielding Catt, Company K, 44th Indiana Infantry.

# A SAD CASE

From the middle of August till the 1st of September there were no deaths in the hospital. On the 14th of September, Richard Swift, of the 44th Indiana, died. The best of care could not save him. I recall one very sad case. Among those who died in my ward was a young German by the name of Gustavus Knoblauch.[70] He had been accidentally wounded just before his regiment left for home. I learned that his folks lived in St. Louis, Mo. so I wrote his mother, informing her of his death, and stating that I had cut a lock of his hair, which I would send her in case she so desired. Some time afterwards I received two letters from his sister, from which I make the following quotations:

> How can I express the gratitude which we all feel towards you, who, though a perfect stranger, showed so much kindness to a dying soldier? Alas! The mother for whom you cut that precious lock of hair is no more! One month from the day the terrible news reached us she breathed her last. She never found out why her darling son did not return; why he was not here to receive her blessing. Oh, the terrible anguish of those days! When she called for him, and we tried to appear cheerful, and our hearts were torn with grief. The recollection of those days will never fade from our memory. Four years and a half our noble brother had fought for his adopted country: had suffered all imaginable ills without ever complaining, and when on the point of returning to gladden our desolate home he was swept away. Two years before another dear brother was torn from our side, also a sacrifice to his country. Both died away from home and friends; both were interred by strangers. Many prayers have been sent up to Him for your welfare, who so kindly ministered to our brother and others.

By the 19th of September several of the wards had been closed. There were but four patients left in the hospital, and it did not seem necessary for us to remain any longer. The surgeon in charge had given us permission to leave, and our trunks being packed, we once more said good-by, and Miss Tuttle and I took our final leave of Chattanooga. I returned at once to my friends, having been actively engaged in this hospital work for four years and two months.

Miss Tuttle returned to her home in Ohio. The last I heard of her she was teaching freedmen in Texas. Miss Bell, now Mrs. Dr. Stubbs, resides in Philadelphia, Pa. Miss Chamberlain, now Mrs.

---

70. Gustavus A. Knoblauch, Company G, 2nd Missouri Cavalry.

Eccleston, is engaged in teaching in South America. Miss Dysart resides in Tipton, Pa. Mrs. Hall, now Mrs. Barry, resides in San Francisco, Cal.

During all the time I was in the hospitals I kept no journal. These reminiscences have been gleaned from letters I sent home, and I realize how very meager they are, for during much of the four years there was no time for even letter writing. Many other interesting incidents might have been given. In one instance I referred to the death of one of whose fate his company were ignorant. During all these years they had remained in ignorance of what had become of him.

Since I commenced writing these reminiscences I have received quite a number of letters from those who were in the hospitals and their friends. It is pleasant to be remembered by those to whom I ministered so long ago, and trusting that these articles have not been without interest to your readers, I now bring my story to a close.

[THE END]

*Harriet Dada.*

**About the author:**

Mr. Raus was born in Cortland, New York and graduated from the State University of New York at Cortland. He has written a number of books and articles on Civil War subjects including the Thomas publication, *A Generation on the March: The Union Army at Gettysburg*. He lives in The Plains, Virginia.

---

**Titles of similar interest from Thomas Publications:**

*A Vast Army of Women*
    by Lynda Sudlow
*A Woman of Honor: Dr. Mary Walker & the Civil War*
    by Mercedes Graf
*Exile to Sweet Dixie: The Story of Euphemia Goldsborough*
    by Eillen Conklin
*Ties of the Past: Gettysburg Diaries of Salome Myers Stewart*
    by Sarah Thomas
*White Roses: Stories of Women Nurses in the Civil War*
    by Rebecca Larson
*Women at Gettysburg, 1863*
    by Eileen Conklin

---

THOMAS PUBLICATIONS publishes books about the American Colonial era, the Revolutionary War, the Civil War, and other important topics. For a complete list of titles, please visit our website at:

    www.thomaspublications.com

Or write to:
    THOMAS PUBLICATIONS
    P.O. Box 3031
    Gettysburg, Pa. 17325